Praise for

A Faith of Our Own and Jonathan's Work

"Merritt represents a hopeful new current in evangelical America." —*USA Today*

"By broadening evangelicalism's agenda, younger evangelicals like *Jonathan Merritt*...are doing us a favor."
—*The Dallas Morning News*

"Merritt's book provides a rare window into a youth spent in the upper echelons of the Christian Right, all the more illuminating because it's from the hand of a thoughtful critic, which isn't to say a left-wing convert. The story of Merritt's exit from a hard-edged political movement to a more centrist, more complex political place is a potent and timely symbol of the journeys of many young American evangelicals."
—Dan Gilgoff, CNN.com religion editor

"Being a follower of Jesus of Nazareth forces each person to make a choice—which Kingdom and which King will you serve? You can't serve both God's Kingdom and an earthly one. In this book, Jonathan Merritt forces the reader to 'choose this day whom you will serve.' In choosing the right Kingdom and right King, we have the most effect on the one that is passing away. But in choosing the wrong Kingdom and King, we affect neither."
—Cal Thomas, syndicated *USA Today* columnist and Fox News contributor

"[Merritt] writes with humility and clarity. He addresses the political, cultural and biblical assumptions many of us hold."

—*Christianity Today*

"After a wearisome decade where younger Christians welcomed the downfall of the Religious Right, Merritt charts the way forward—helping us imagine a new, constructive way to advance the common good in the public square. *A Faith of Our Own* provides a roadmap for how Christians can engage the future."

—Gabe Lyons, author of *The Next Christians* and founder of Q

"Research shows shifts among younger evangelicals, particularly in regard to their views of social engagement, yet polls and statistics have not told the whole story. Now, in this personal, provocative, and well-written book—part memoir, part manifesto—Merritt lays out his journey and his case. If you want to understand shifts in younger evangelicalism, this book is a must read."   —Ed Stetzer, president of LifeWay Research

"In this provocative book, Merritt again and again challenges Christians to reconsider their comfortable lives and their easy acceptance of either right-wing or left-wing politics as God's way of living their faith in the world. In an engaging, powerful manner, he shows why many young Christians are rethinking the political heritage handed down to them by their elders."

—Steve Monsma, senior research fellow at the Henry Institute for the Study of Christianity and Politics at Calvin College and professor emeritus of political science at Pepperdine University

"For what should it profit a man if he should win the election but lose his own soul? Probably more than anyone else, Jonathan Merritt has effectively tapped into the growing sense among young Christians that while political participation may be noble, overt partisanship can compromise your calling. *A Faith of Our Own* is a must-read for anyone who wants to understand a post–culture war generation of Christians."

—Matt Lewis, *The Daily Caller* senior contributor

"A forceful but loving critique by a gifted young leader of the tragic failures of my generation of evangelicals. Plus a biblically solid, Christ-centered way forward. A must-read."

—Ronald J. Sider, bestselling author of *Rich Christians in an Age of Hunger* and President of Evangelicals for Social Action

"Jonathan Merritt's *A Faith of Our Own* provides the American Church in the twenty-first century the optics and lenses for viable prophetic witness that replaces rancor with civility, animosity with love, and apathy with hope. Merritt represents an entire generation seeking to reconcile sanctification with service without embracing the extremes. This book provides a blueprint that if applied will replace the image of an angry, white evangelical in the public square with a compassionate follower of Christ in the heart of the community."

—Rev. Samuel Rodriguez, president of the National Hispanic Christian Leadership Conference

"Jonathan Merritt is part of a new generation of evangelicals seeking to be kingdom builders rather than culture warriors. He thinks Christians should be salt and light rather than fire and ice. We should listen to him."
—Barry Hankins, author of *Jesus and Gin: Evangelicalism, the Roaring Twenties, and Today's Culture Wars* and professor of history and church-state studies at Baylor University

"In my head, Jonathan Merritt will forever be a hybrid. With one foot on truths that are eons old and the other leaning into the future, he offers a combination of perspectives that is challenging, inspiring and difficult to resist."
—Jonathan Acuff, blogger and author of *Stuff Christians Like*

"With eloquence, wit, and experience, Jonathan illuminates the incongruence between Christian political partisanship and the Gospel of Jesus. Offering profound insight and vision, Jonathan inspires hope that there is a less divisive way for Christians to engage politics and culture—a way that looks more like Jesus, marked by humility, grace, mercy, and respect."
—Phileena Heuertz, author of *Pilgrimage of a Soul: Contemplative Spirituality for the Active Life*

"Jonathan Merritt gives us a personal and intriguing guidebook for Christian participation in the public square. As a church leader involved in the moral causes of our time, he helps us all understand how political participation can be yet another way to exercise our faith in Christ. This is a fresh look from a young leader!"
—Joel Hunter, author and pastor of Northland Church

"With candor and wisdom, Jonathan Merritt points the way toward a new civic engagement that reflects authentically Christian values. Tearing down sacred cows that served as idols to a previous generation, he offers insight into a way forward that encompasses a hopeful future for the role of faith in American culture. With *A Faith of Our Own*, Merritt reveals the courage to speak bold truth in love for the good of the Church."

—Soong-Chan Rah, author of *The Next Evangelicalism: Freeing the Church from Western Cultural Captivity* and Milton B. Engebretson Associate Professor of Church Growth and Evangelism at North Park Theological Seminary

A
FAITH
OF OUR
OWN

A
FAITH
OF OUR
OWN

FOLLOWING JESUS BEYOND
THE CULTURE WARS

JONATHAN MERRITT

Faith
Words

NEW YORK • NASHVILLE

Unless otherwise indicated, Scriptures are quoted from
The Holy Bible, New International Version®. Copyright © 1973,
1978, 1984, 2011 by the International Bible Society. Used by
permission of Zondervan Publishing House. All rights reserved.

Scripture quotations marked NLT are taken from *Holy Bible*, New Living
Translation®. Copyright © 1996. Used by permission of Tynsdale House
Publishers, Inc., Wheaton, Illinois. All rights reserved.

FaithWords
Hachette Book Group
237 Park Avenue
New York, NY 10017

Printed in the United States of America

www.faithwords.com
FaithWords is a division of Hachette Book Group, Inc.
The FaithWords name and logo are trademarks of Hachette Book Group, Inc.

First Edition: May 2012
10 9 8 7 6 5 4 3 2 1

RRD-C

The publisher is not responsible for websites (or their content)
that are not owned by the publisher.

Library of Congress Cataloging-in-Publication Data
Merritt, Jonathan.
   A faith of our own : following Jesus beyond the culture wars / Jonathan
Merritt. — 1st ed.
       p. cm.
   ISBN 978-0-446-55723-8
   1. Christianity and politics—United States.   2. Culture conflict—United
States.   I. Title.
   BR115.P7M514 2012
   261.70973—dc23

                                                      2011047072

To a generation of journeyers.
We walk together.

If you would attain to what you are not yet, you must always be displeased by what you are. For where you are pleased with yourself there you have remained. Keep adding, keep walking, keep advancing.

—St. Augustine

Contents

Foreword

Six years ago when I became a Christian—in some ways, completely against my will or wishes—the first thought I had was, "I can't be a Christian because I don't want to be a Republican!"

I was a lifelong liberal who had worked in the Clinton White House, on various Democratic campaigns, and was quite at home with my political worldview. I didn't want to associate with the conservative politics that so many Christians hold. I was also uncomfortable with what I perceived as the anti-gay, anti-intellectual, judgmental perspectives in the community.

Why would I associate conservative politics or these other behaviors with Christianity? Some would argue that it's the media that have painted Christianity—especially of the orthodox or evangelical breed—in a bad light, and that it's unfair to use such a broad brush to describe Christians. This is partly true, but the longer I'm a part of the community, the more I realize that Christians bear the bulk of the responsibility for the current image of Christianity.

At the wedding of a friend a few years ago, a conservative woman came up to me and said, "I watch you on TV all the time and sometimes I just want to slap you! I've thought many times of sending you a letter saying, 'If you knew the Lord, you would be a Republican.'"

She almost fell out of her chair when I calmly said, "I do know the Lord, and I'm a Democrat."

This did not compute.

I'm often asked, "How can you be a Democrat and a Christian?" which puzzles me beyond belief. Nowhere in the Bible is there a mandate to be a Republican, or to support low taxes or, say, the war in Iraq, which I opposed from the beginning. And for all the conflation of patriotism and being a good Christian, I'm sorry to tell people that God is actually not an American. He created and cares about everyone in the world, not just Americans.

Whether it's Jerry Falwell blaming feminists, pagans, and gays for the 9/11 attacks, or Christian pastors and leaders openly aligning themselves with the Republican Party to oppose health-care reform and immigration reform in the name of Jesus, Christianity has a major problem. Yes, it is an image problem. But more importantly it's a problem of corrupting the gospel with petty politics and partisan ideology. It's creating divisiveness within a community that is supposed to be known by our love.

By the way, the solution is not to corrupt the gospel with left-wing views either. Some Christians pursue this path, and the result is equally damaging. Weeks after Hurricane Katrina in 2005, I attended Abyssinian Baptist Church in Harlem only to hear the Rev. Calvin Butts tell the congregation, "George Bush hates black people," because of the federal government's insufficient response to the catastrophe.

Both sides are responsible for corrupting the Christian gospel with partisan political views. I know firsthand how wonderful Christians can be—most of my closest friends are Christians—but the idea that loving Jesus means voting for a certain party still lingers.

I became a Christian while attending a wonderful church in New York City. Redeemer Presbyterian is led by Tim Keller, called the "thinking man's evangelical" by *New York Magazine*. Keller is one of those orthodox pastors who believes his job is to share the gospel, not slam the Democratic Party or parrot Republican talking points. But even with such a pastor leading my church, I had a hard time finding other congregants who shared my political worldview, though occasionally I would sense I had met one and would whisper, "Wait, are you a Democrat?" We usually became fast friends.

Looking for a smaller church with more community, I started attending Trinity Grace Church, led by a young pastor named Jon Tyson. The bulk of the congregation was in their twenties or early thirties. There I encountered something disarmingly different. While the church teachings were orthodox, the congregants were politically diverse. Barack Obama supporters abounded alongside George Bush and John McCain fans. While there were plenty of attendees who I'm sure voted Republican, it wasn't of the knee-jerk "all Christians vote Republican" kind. One could sense that people chose candidates based on their values, not simply their political party.

I started to encounter more and more people, including those who identified as conservatives, who were frustrated with the Pat Robertsons and James Dobsons of the world, who they felt gave evangelicals a bad name by their constant politicizing or intolerant comments.

It gave me hope.

Through this church community I was connected to many interesting thinkers, including the author of this book, Jonathan Merritt. He is another person who gives me hope. Jonathan envisions a future where the Christian Church is not Republican or Democrat, but rather faithful to the teachings of Jesus Christ—a future that is quickly approaching.

While he and I don't see eye to eye on everything politically, we agree on one thing: Christians must move away from the partisan, power-seeking, polemical expressions of religion to a more Jesus-driven faith. I'm excited by the movement under way in the church—led largely by the younger generation—to decouple it from partisan politics and focus on living out the gospel.

The world needs such a movement, and this book comes not a moment too soon.

Kirsten Powers
Fox News political analyst and *New York Post* columnist

Read This First

The slip fell out of my wallet and fluttered, like a down feather, to the floor. I bent over and felt the waitress's eyes follow me as I reached for the narrow, folded paper. What might be mistaken for a receipt was an invaluable reminder I take with me everywhere I go.

I first began carrying it a few years ago during a struggle with my faith. I was trying to reconcile the Jesus I was encountering in the New Testament with the one I, and so many Americans, claimed to follow. In the Bible, I kept meeting a Jesus who was radical and revolutionary. But many "Christians" I knew worshiped a domesticated Savior—one whose message was easy to swallow and even easier to live by. Their Jesus hated the same people they hated, voted like they did, and made few difficult demands. I developed a nagging sense that the Bible's Jesus might not care for the Jesus many Americans believed in.

I confessed my uneasiness over dinner with an old schoolmate. As a good friend does, he spoke less than he listened. When I finished my lament, he offered one piece of advice. He told me to purchase a copy of *Faust*, by Johann Wolfgang von Goethe, recognized by many as the greatest German writer who ever lived. He told me to place my frustrations on the shelf for a few days while I read it, or rather let it read me. I agreed.

The next day, I brought home a translation of the heavy tome and dove headfirst into its pages. The plot of this poetic play revolves around a scholar and sorcerer, Dr. Faust, who exchanges his soul for human knowledge. Goethe's rhythmic words are lush and hypnotizing, and I was mesmerized from the first act. In the opening scene, the character Wagner claims he possesses great knowledge but desires to know everything. Faust's response caught me off guard:

> That which you have received as heritage, now rediscover for yourself and thus you will make it your own.

I stopped, giving the words time to settle.

Then I read them again.

And again.

I wrote them down and tucked the wisdom into my wallet.

Faust's words felt like a signpost pointing me forward in my spiritual journey. As a follower of Jesus, I can cherish the faith of my father and grandfathers. But I also need to take hold of it myself.

A writer friend of mine, John, had a similar experience a few years ago while sitting by a campfire. Having grown up in a Christian home, he'd practiced the faith of his parents, but it was just that—his parents' faith. As flickering flames illuminated the night sky, he asked God to make Himself real to him. And God did.

An insatiable desire to read the Bible welled up from his innermost parts, and John began to devour the Scriptures. Old passages took on new life, and John experienced the Jesus who *is*, not the Jesus he'd seen from afar through his parents' religion. He began serving others, praying with others, and started a Bible study for young Christians. The faith of his father was now his.

Maybe John discovered something different or perhaps he had willingly accepted the same faith, now that it was not forced on him. He rediscovered a faith that had been handed to him, but now it was his own.

In the sixteenth chapter of Matthew's Gospel, Jesus asks Peter who people believe Jesus is. Peter replies that there is some confusion among the masses. Some think Jesus is John the Baptist, others Elijah, and still others say He may be Jeremiah or another prophet who's come back to life.

None of these answers was correct, and Jesus asks Peter, "But what about you? Who do you say I am?"

This is a defining question posed to every generation and culture.[1] Jesus was not just speaking to Peter. Each successive generation of Christians must give their own answer to Jesus' frank inquiry. *Who do we say Jesus is?* Our answer cannot be drawn from what others are saying about Jesus or what our parents taught us about Him. We must stare Jesus in the face and offer our own response.

Peter seems to know precisely who Jesus is: "You are the Messiah, the Son of the living God."[2]

Peter, the first-century Jew and former fisherman who has given up everything to become Christ's disciple, believes Jesus to be the One for whom Israel has been waiting for millennia. He is the Savior; He is God's Son; He is everything.

Like Peter, every generation must see Jesus with their own eyes and learn to follow Him in their own way, even though He is "the same yesterday and today and forever."[3] Though the Savior looks different to many—a father, a friend, a shepherd— He is still unchanging and so are His precepts. We must have an encounter with this ageless Jesus for our own time.

"Each successive epoch," Albert Schweitzer said, "found its own thoughts in Jesus, which was indeed the only way it could make him live."[4]

First-century Christians in Israel wrestled with Jesus, the Jewish rabbi and Messiah. Second-century Roman Christians preached Jesus as the King of Kings who, unlike Caesar, was Lord of all. In the eighth and ninth centuries, Christians' embrace of Jesus as the true image of God spawned new forms of art, architecture, and religious icons. In the Middle Ages, Christians wrestled with Jesus as the crucified God. During the Protestant Reformation, they discovered a Jesus who justifies humankind with sacrificial grace. Christians of the Enlightenment embraced Jesus, the God of reason, while Christians during the American civil rights movement recognized Jesus as the great liberator.[5]

Each of these images is a crystallization of who Jesus is.

Throughout history, however, Christians have often let culture, rather than Christ, define their faith. This might certainly be true of the Crusaders' Jesus, for example, who was a God of war and domination. Christians always face the temptation to depict Jesus in accordance with their own character[6] and cast Him in an image that best suits their worldly goals.

The Christianity I often witnessed growing up seemed to be engaged in a political struggle for control of a nation in "moral decline." The answer to "Who do you say Jesus is?" was pietistic and political. Jesus wanted us to take back our country for Him rather than leave everything behind and follow.

Raised in a conservative family with ties to many leaders in the so-called Religious Right, I thought faithful followship of Jesus meant defeating liberals. I assumed most people felt like my community did—that a cantankerous minority of secular humanists were attempting to chase Jesus out of God-blessed America. Our duty was to resist them.

As a young adult, I discovered that Christians on the left saw my community as revisionist historians who desired to transform America into an oppressive theocracy. Their Jesus didn't care much for us, and ours didn't like them either. Both sides had accepted a faith that seemed more shaped by American culture than by the Christ I kept encountering in the Bible.

Philosopher Jacques Ellul once said, "It seems as though politics is the Church's worst problem. It is her constant temptation, the occasion of her greatest disasters, the trap continually set for her by the Prince of this World."[7] But Ellul is only partially right. Politics itself is not the problem. Foolish participation in politics is what gets the church into trouble. It divides a community for which God desires unity and forces us to lose site of the reason we live and move and breathe.

That's why much of American Christianity—in the words of former Bush speechwriter and *Washington Post* columnist Michael Gerson—is in a moment of "head-snapping" change in which our wholesale participation in America's culture wars is being reevaluated.[8] Today's believers are rediscovering Christianity and searching for a more Jesus-shaped faith. They aren't leaving the public square altogether, but Christians of all ages—particularly the younger ones—are now rediscovering their faith and the One upon whom that faith is built. They are weary of the partisanship, the struggle for power. They want to go beyond the ballot box and *do* something concrete about our many problems.

Today's Christians are returning to the Bible and glimpsing Jesus with fresh eyes and uncovering a faith that transcends the culture wars. They want a faith that isn't just politically active, but one that transforms life. They believe we can call a truce in the culture wars while remaining faithful to Christ. In fact, they believe faithfulness requires such a cease-fire.

Every time I look at the crinkled paper that rests among the receipts in my wallet, Goethe's fading words cry out. The old poet whispers to a new generation of Christians, beckoning them to embrace the faith that's been handed down to them while making it their own.

Those in whose wake we now walk discerned how the faith should go forward in a time of cultural change and moral decline. A new generation must now decide how to go forward in our day. As I survey the Christian landscape, I see many who are staring down their Savior. They are answering the "who do you say" question as they follow Jesus beyond the culture wars.

This is their story.

And mine.

ONE

Breakfast with Falwell

It's interesting that nowadays politicians want to talk about moral issues, and bishops want to talk politics.
—SIR HUMPHREY APPLEBY FROM
YES, PRIME MINISTER

My restless legs shook under a table in the Lynchburg, Virginia, IHOP. I sat in a booth facing the entrance, my eyes fixed on the door. My stomach churned with nervous excitement and a splash of scared silly. Next to me, my dad sat quietly—calmer than I, but a bit anxious as well. We both knew the significance of this moment: I was about to meet Jerry Falwell for the first time.

Depending on one's upbringing, that name may not conjure up the same emotions that it did in me in 1999 at the age of 17. For some, the name "Jerry Falwell" incites a roll of the eyes or anger. But I was raised to revere and respect Dr. Falwell, the veritable founder of the Religious Right. I saw him as a paragon of principle, a crusader for common Christians. These sentiments were reinforced throughout my life, since I had grown up in the inner sanctum of evangelicalism.

My father was a prominent Southern Baptist minister who expected us to be in church four times weekly, twice on Sundays. As his church size and influence grew, politicians extended invitations for fund-raising dinners and public events where our family would follow in tow—his smiling entourage of support.

Today, a picture hangs in Dad's office of him with me, my brother, and President George H. W. Bush. It's an emblem of the place I grew up. The Deep South. A world of fiery religion and frenzied politics. A world in which the two are often indistinguishable.

Within months of this meeting, Dad would be elected president of the Southern Baptist Convention (SBC), the largest Protestant denomination in America, which boasted 16 million members. Dr. Falwell knew the importance of such things, so he asked Dad to bring me up to his college—Liberty University—for a good old-fashioned sales pitch.

As the door swung open, my eyes widened. Power clung to his frame like his pressed oxford and three-button blazer. The preacher's silver hair and genuine smile contributed to his jovial persona, but Jerry Falwell always meant business. He owned the room.

"This must be the future Liberty student," he said snatching my hand and giving a firm squeeze. "James, we need to get this young man in Lynchburg."

"I'm doing the best I can to convince him," Dad responded.

Dr. Falwell sat down and motioned for our server. Without opening a menu, he rattled off his behest. The precision of his order told me this wasn't his first visit to the International House of Pancakes, and the way he bantered about with the waitstaff indicated that it wouldn't be his last.

Dad and I followed with our selections, and then the time arrived to address the reasons for our meeting. Dr. Falwell explained why Liberty was the university for me. He was building Liberty to become "the Notre Dame for evangelicals," and it had everything a Christian could ask for—NCAA sports, conservative education, a student body where the girls outnumbered the boys. (Later on, I felt like he had exaggerated on the last point, but that's a separate issue.)

"That's why you need to be here next year, son. There's no greater place on earth for training champions for Christ," he said.

Dr. Falwell finished his sales pitch knowing he'd closed the deal. He'd given this talk a thousand times before. Then he turned to Dad, who, as a member of the Liberty board of trustees, asked about the school's finances. Dr. Falwell remarked they were stable, but could be better.

"Enough about Liberty, Dr. Falwell," Dad said. "How's your ministry going?"

The reverend's jovial smile went somber, and he leaned in closely.

"James, we've got the numbers. We've got the resources. We've got the leadership," he said. "I've spoken to conservative Christians in churches all across this country, and they know what is at stake. We've got to get serious about Jesus, and we need to call this nation back to its roots. It's time to stand for what is right."

But then he added, "We've got to get our folks to the polls next year, and we need to do a better job telling people what will happen if liberal Democrats remain in control of the White House. *We must save this nation!*"

My brow furrowed. Even a 17-year-old realizes when someone's answer doesn't match the question. Dad asked Dr. Falwell about his ministry, and Falwell answered with a strategy for acquiring political power.

Jerry Falwell believed that our country was at a critical point in its history and that the responsibility to act rested on the Christian community. The stakes were high, and we couldn't afford to lose. So strong were his feelings that he devoted a considerable amount of his time and ministry resources to leading the effort. With the resolve of Admiral Farragut—"Damn the torpedoes, full speed ahead"—he was prepared to fight at all costs.

* * *

The preacher *was* not and *is* not alone in his approach to faith, politics, and culture. A conflict is raging, and the spoils are the rights to control and shape our nation and its policies. Unlike traditional military conflicts, this skirmish produces no physical casualties, but often results in the deaths of characters and reputations. Untrusting eyes stare across battle lines, with progressives crouched on one side and traditionalists on the other.

Constituencies are mobilized, opinions are polarized, and divisions run deep.

Turn on the television and you'll lay witness to raging war in stereo and Technicolor. One needs Tylenol to absorb the pounding pundits. Behar busts on O'Reilly, O'Reilly screams about Matthews, Matthews gripes about Hannity, Hannity fumes at Maddow, and Maddow can't stop giving that same, tired stump speech about Limbaugh. It's maddening.

They will occasionally stop to do an interview or two, but their guests are just as abrasive. Whether it's a politician insulting an opponent or a "strategist" shouting talking points, the noise blurs together into one angry mess. Worst of all, nobody seems to be saying anything!

Turning the television off won't solve the problem. Radio fills with the same nonsense, just louder. And if you mute the radio, you're still assaulted by billboards, bumper stickers, and yard signs waving their collective hands and imploring you to choose a side.

Welcome to America's culture war.

The term "culture war" originated in the 1960s, but James Davison Hunter popularized the term in his 1992 book *Culture Wars: The Struggle to Define America*. According to Hunter, the passionate fights to shape the nation's stance and policy on contentious political issues are not disconnected, but part of a larger conflict rooted in our moral imaginations:

America is in the midst of a culture war that has had and will continue to have reverberations not only within public policy but within the lives of ordinary Americans everywhere. I define cultural conflict very simply as political and social hostility rooted in different systems of moral understanding. The end to which these hostilities tend is the domination of one cultural and moral ethos over all others.[1]

In other words, Bill O'Reilly shouting about immigration and Al Franken whining about "lying liars" aren't secluded opinions piercing America's airwaves but the crossfire of two field officers from camps with radically different systems of moral thought. Abortion clinic protestors and anti-war demonstrators aren't isolated pockets of resistance to individual issues, but rather the manifestations of conflicting cultural values.

Like a fish caught in a gill net, the Christian community has become enmeshed in this struggle. News shows feature pastors as pundits who offer opinions on everything from health care to tax reform, constitutional law to American history. Religious practitioners garner a seat at the table, and their massive followings cement them there.

As a senior in high school, I was unaware of the war going on around me—a war in which I was unwittingly entangled. This was the world in which I was raised, the only one I'd ever known. When I met Dr. Falwell in IHOP that day, I was in the presence of a five-star general of the culture wars. A staunch traditionalist and valiant conservative, he had served on the front lines for more than two decades when we met. Dr. Falwell and other Christian leaders like him were constructing a politico-religious machine long before I ordered the blueberry pancakes. And masses were following them into the fray.

During my formative years, others warned me that modernist liberals sought to obliterate all notions of God and destroy our precious way of life. Our family, our faith, our entire nation was locked in a struggle that Christians could not afford to lose. I responded by hunkering down in the cultural trenches. I consumed a steady diet of conservative writers like Ann Coulter and trained myself to combat the slander of godless liberals. I took my cues from vetted figures in the Religious Right, my trusted guides in the cultural conflict.

Such entrenchment was necessary if I hoped to honor our Lord by fighting off His political enemies. I never considered otherwise. After all, if one walked into a Southern evangelical church during the 1980s or '90s, being greeted with both a handshake and a Christian Coalition voter's guide wasn't the slightest bit abnormal.[2] In the conservative vortex where I spent my incubator years, fighting the culture wars was a Christian's duty.

* * *

Is this what it means to follow Jesus in the twenty-first century? Is this what it looks like to pursue the kingdom-come life he spoke so often about? Memorize some talking points and vote into office the politicians who promise to favor us and our agendas?

I'm unconvinced. I've spent many hours of my adult life combing the New Testament Gospels to understand why Jesus seemed so much less engaged in politics than I was. The Israel known by Christ was as bitterly divided as America is today. The Jewish people were essentially slaves to the Roman government. The Romans determined their living conditions and extracted exorbitant taxes to build Roman-style cities that threatened the survival of Israel's culture. The Jewish people in the first century were terrorized by a government that was more oppressive than Saddam Hussein's, more uncooperative than Kim Jong Il's, and as imperialistic as Adolf Hitler's.

Just before Jesus' birth, Roman armies rolled through Galilee, burning down villages and killing innocents. Any who resisted their rule were tortured and often executed to deter mass rebellion. Sometime around or after Jesus' birth, the Roman general Varus gathered the rebels in and around Jesus' hometown and crucified about 2,000 men.[3] One might have argued that during the first century, Israel's greatest need was political revolution.

When Jesus began His public ministry, the Jewish people were looking for a warrior, a conqueror, a new King David. If there was ever a time when a "war on terror" was needed, it was Jesus' lifetime. But Jesus showed little interest in sanctifying the state. In fact, He rarely acknowledged the Roman government under which He lived. Even when Satan offered to give Him authority over "all the kingdoms of the world," Jesus said, "no thanks." He had something else in mind.

In researching the way the Romans treated the Jews around the time of Jesus' birth, I found myself wishing Jesus had intervened. After chasing out the temple money changers, couldn't He have chased out the Roman oppressors? Jesus was God, after all. But He refuses to fit the mold I want to make for Him.

At first reading of the Gospels, Jesus seems almost unconcerned with political engagement. Sure, His teachings had profound political implications, but He wasn't interested in organizing a constituency to fight political battles.

I could not at first understand why He refused to mobilize His followers to take up the sword and return Israel to her glory. Instead of fighting *against* the Romans, He fought *for* the Jews. Rather than shedding blood, He promoted peace. Instead of inflicting pain on the oppressor, He offered healing to the oppressed. Rather than marginalizing those who opposed Him, He accepted those who were marginalized. Jesus could have spent His time schmoozing with the political elite, but instead He chose to dwell among the poor.

Rather than giving political speeches, Jesus talked obsessively about this idea called "kingdom."[4] He spoke about it more than anything else, and it was the central element of His good news. He pursued, preached, and embodied this message. "The time has come," Jesus often said. "The kingdom of God is at hand." According to the New Testament, Jesus ushered in the kingdom of God, bringing the good news with Him to earth and spreading its seeds through His work among us. Those who follow Him are supposed to desire it, live it, and partner with God to continue promoting it in Jesus' physical absence.

But what is the kingdom of God? What does it look like and how does one pursue it? How we answer has huge implications for how we engage faith, culture, and politics.

Like a physical kingdom, God's kingdom is the time and place in which He reigns over all things. God's attributes saturate every cubic inch of his kingdom. Peace reigns in God's kingdom because God is peace. Love is supreme in God's kingdom because God is love. Mercy is palpable in God's kingdom because God is the ultimate mercy giver. Righteousness is endless in God's kingdom because the King's holiness has spilled out onto everything. For this reason, Jesus' most comprehensive description of what kingdom citizens look like includes peacemakers, the meek, and those who crave righteousness like their next meal.[5]

The Bible asserts that the seeds of this kingdom were already planted by the Great Sower, Jesus. Christ's death on the cross is bringing everything under His supremacy.[6] Though the kingdom will not fully blossom until He returns to reign, humans can experience it right now. For this reason, Jesus taught that the kingdom is both a coming reality[7] and already here.[8]

If the kingdom of God is the end game, the end goal, the prize Christians must pursue, we must only look at our pursuits to distill out our definition of the kingdom. Culture warriors take the Bible's vast teachings on God's kingdom and shrink ray it to fit their specific purposes. When Christians devote their lives exclusively to the construction of an earthly power, when their mission sounds like a campaign strategy, it's clear that they believe God's kingdom can be reached by political victories.

Many on the Christian left speak as if the kingdom of God entails implementing a "social justice" agenda in Washington, getting our troops off the battlefield, and obliterating the reign of the Christian Right. For those on the right, the kingdom amounts to voting Christians into office, making abortion and gay marriage illegal, reinstating prayer in public schools, and posting the Ten Commandments in courthouses.[9] When either of these agendas becomes the ultimate measure of faithfulness, the kingdom of God is supplanted by our political strategies.

Russell Moore, dean of theology at Southern Baptist Theological Seminary, has said, "The failure of evangelical politics is often, at root, the failure of an evangelical theology of the Kingdom."[10] Christians must investigate what pursuing God's kingdom means before they embark on political engagement.

Linking God's kingdom with puny political platforms robs it of the majesty, holiness, vastness, and stunning beauty that more accurately demonstrate who God is.[11] The result of a political ideology divorced from a political theology is a public engagement that often oversteps, overreaches, and underwhelms skeptical non-believers. Perhaps that explains why so few choose to submit to the King in their hearts and lives today. If followers of Jesus misunderstand the kingdom, they misunderstand their mission.

Understanding what Jesus taught about the kingdom forces us to challenge our assumptions about how Christians engage the public square. The kingdom informs believers how high a premium they should place on personal political agendas. It shows them what faith looks like in our current age.

* * *

Before I left Lynchburg, I shook the preacher's hand, but I was unable to shake his comments. As our car rumbled back from the James River Valley to metropolitan Atlanta, I thought long and hard about what Dr. Falwell had said. Impressed by his presence and passion, I shared many of the same sentiments.

Dr. Falwell said we needed to get serious about Jesus. I wanted to get serious about Jesus. He said we needed to call our nation back to its roots. I wanted our nation to return to its roots. Dr. Falwell said it was time to stand for what is right. I wanted to stand for what was right.

But even then, my teenage mind wasn't sure that he had effectively navigated how faith should mingle with politics.

Less than one year after my breakfast with Jerry Falwell, I returned to Lynchburg as a freshman at Liberty University. Homesick and formative, I dipped my toe into the waters of the evangelical super-school. Three times each week I attended a mandatory convocation (code word for "chapel") where students listened to a sampling of America's best evangelical preachers—interrupted on occasion by conservative spokespersons like former congressman J. C. Watts and Sean Hannity, who would "preach" slightly different sermons.

On Sundays, I attended Falwell's Thomas Road Baptist Church, where I always became flush with emotion. I enjoyed the fanfare and feeling a part of something significant. However, I left most Sundays with an emptiness from the lack of theological substance that I had come to expect from church attendance.

A typical Sunday service might showcase the reverend standing behind the pulpit telling stories about his appearances that week on *Meet the Press* or *Politically Incorrect with Bill Maher*. On a particularly raucous Sunday, he might also endorse a few candidates or talk about an upcoming vote in Congress. His strong statements were often met with a cheer from the crowd.

As I shuffled out of the sanctuary each week, I rarely felt as if I had encountered the Divine. I usually felt as if I had just attended a political rally. On several occasions, my friends and I would spend Sunday lunch trying to decipher whether the good news of Jesus or even a single spiritual truth had been communicated in church that day.

I discovered later that Dr. Falwell's ministry had not always been marked by such overt political partisanship. Like most fundamentalists and many evangelicals in the mid-twentieth century, he was a cultural separatist who believed that the world was inherently evil and that God's people should avoid intimate interaction with its institutions and constituencies.

In 1965, the reverend stood tall and proud to preach a sermon titled "Ministers and Marches" that he regretted later in life. He was troubled by a movement of clergy who were marching for civil rights and embracing political activism. Speaking to dissuade these clergy from setting up shop in the public square, he said,

> Believing the Bible as I do, I would find it impossible to stop preaching the pure saving gospel of Jesus Christ and begin doing anything else—including fighting communism, or participating in civil rights reforms....Preachers are not called to be politicians but to be soul winners....Nowhere are we commissioned to reform the externals. The gospel does not clean up the outside but rather regenerates the inside.[12]

Dr. Falwell lamented this sermon for a couple of reasons. His words were soaked in racist overtones for which he later showed penitence. Also, in just 15 years he would found the

Moral Majority, a Christian mobilization effort that would rush headlong into political engagement. Four decades later, the sermon was a lasting indictment against the person he became.

I was privileged to be with Jerry Falwell many more times in the years that followed, and I know he always meant well. But I believe he was often misguided. I've been unpacking his comments during that breakfast for more than a decade, and I'm still trying to answer questions generated by that experience.

A moment of clarity came after graduating from Liberty when I first read C. S. Lewis's *Screwtape Letters*. This classic book recounts a fictional correspondence between Wormwood, a demon-in-training, and Screwtape, his more experienced uncle. Like any demon-uncle, Screwtape takes the tutelage of young Wormwood seriously. Toward the end of the book, he advises Wormwood on how to destroy a Christian:

> Let him begin by treating patriotism…as a part of his religion. Then let him, under the influence of partisan spirit, come to regard it as the most important part. Then quietly and gradually nurse him on to the stage at which the religion becomes merely a part of the "cause," in which Christianity is valued chiefly because of the excellent arguments it can produce….Once you have made the world an end, and faith a means, you have almost won your man, and it makes very little difference what kind of worldly end he is pursuing.[13]

Treating patriotism as part of religion? The influence of the partisan spirit? Religion as merely part of a "cause?" What

Lewis was writing sounded like much of what I'd experienced growing up in the Christian South.

Looking back, I realize that so many Christians on both the right and the left value their faith as a tool of a "greater cause." Religion has become, in many cases, a person's political credentials. The partisan spirit of which Lewis speaks has seduced many well-meaning believers, and once this spirit's fingers are firmly around their necks, it makes very little difference what end they are pursuing. At that point, faith has become a means to an end and no longer an end in itself.

TWO

Journey to Montreat

The tendency to claim God as an ally for our partisan value and ends is the source of all religious fanaticism.
— REINHOLD NIEBUHR

Imagine a stereotypical Southern Baptist church in the South, and you have envisioned the theater of my childhood. Red brick buildings huddle behind a grand façade of Corinthian columns that, like the deltoids of Colossus, appear to hold up the mammoth white steeple. More than a sanctuary and office space, First Baptist Church of Snellville, Georgia, is architecture and history.

I spent countless days and nights there, but it never seemed to get old. First Baptist was the type of church you wanted to belong to. From Christmas programs to community-wide firework shows, something big always seemed to be happening. Inside, children ran through the halls while their parents chatted with friends. Families dined at the local Mexican restaurant after Sunday night services. Our congregation was energetic and vibrant.

We were also unashamedly conservative. Crowds of "Bible-believers" flocked to our sanctuary each week for a thunderous concert by our robed choir and intense preaching that beckoned all who heard to choose sides—holiness or sinfulness, eternity with God or eternity in isolated torment. We were a church that "would never water down the truth" and wasn't "afraid to call sin 'sin.'" As Dad used to remind us, "Right is right even if everyone is against it, and wrong is wrong even if everyone is for it."

Our conservative theology matched our politics. We'd publicly recognize Republican candidates who stopped by during a "church tour." Democratic candidates needed not apply. In the late 1980s, we invited Col. Oliver North to speak; in the early 1990s, I remember church members wearing Bush-Quayle pins on their lapels during Sunday services. In the halls, I once heard a conversation about "that godless Michael Dukakis" who, if elected, was going to let violent prisoners free. I had a nightmare that night that he had won the election and that one of those freed prisoners broke into our house.

When Bill Clinton became president in 1994, many Christians were apoplectic. President Clinton opposed everything they championed and championed everything they opposed. Conservative Christians had fully melded with the Republican Party by then and had been in control of the White House for 12 years, although not much progress had been made on the cornerstone "Christian" issues—no prayer in school, no abortion ban, no halt to the so-called gay agenda. But that didn't seem to matter. They had tasted power, and now they craved the savor.

"Presidents have a kind of political bank account in American minds," A. M. Rosenthal once wrote in the *New York Times*.

"When a President takes an important step, or ducks one, each of us makes a mental deposit or withdrawal according to our political tastes."[1]

Before he stepped foot into the White House, President Clinton withdrew all the money Republican Christians never gave him, and now he deserved wrath or, worse, impeachment. Clinton became public enemy number one among the faithful, the symbol of everything that was wrong with our morally failing nation.

Our congregants loved it when Clinton wandered into Dad's sermons. Even a passing reference to the unnamed "men who have no respect for the Oval Office" was often met with applause. One Sunday, Dad got heated about a hot-button issue and, in a moment of emotion, called Clinton "an idiot." Many in the crowd responded with laughter and an a capella chorus of "amens," but Dad knew the comment was a mistake.

Though Dad is a proud conservative, he also has great reverence for his calling as a pastor. Unlike some, Dad always viewed the pulpit as a sacred platform for preaching the gospel that should be respected. Reasonable and principled, he knew he must apologize.

The next Sunday, after having spent the week in a state of conviction, Dad stood to ask for forgiveness.

"Last week, I called our president an 'idiot' in the pulpit of this church," he said. "I need to apologize to you. I'm sorry. Even if I disagree with the man, I should always show respect for the office."

To me, that was one of Dad's shining moments as a pastor. Responding in kind when threatened or offended is natural. Apologizing after going too far is difficult. Watching Dad admit his wrongdoing showed that he didn't just spout off aphorisms about doing the right thing; he lived by them.

The experience also revealed how partisan many in the church have become. Thousands attended the Sunday services at First Baptist Church in a given week, but I don't remember even a single person walking out the day Dad misspoke. He received no angry letters or complaints. Nothing indicated that anyone sitting in the service felt it was the slightest bit inappropriate. The silence was telling. In the eyes of many congregants, attacking this liberal Democrat from the pulpit was suitable and proper. The bright light of partisanship blinds the eyes of those who refuse to turn away.

•　•　•

Pollster Frank Luntz notes the predictable partisanship of religious people in America. "If I identify myself as a Republican or a Democrat, it tells the listener much less about me than if they know my religion," he writes. "Consequently, knowing their religion and how often they attend church virtually guarantees you know their electoral preference."[2]

Former Christian Coalition executive director and senior official of the Bush-Cheney campaign Ralph Reed attended the Southern Baptist Convention's annual meeting in 2004 to enlist pastors in the reelection effort. Had Reed been working for Kerry-Lieberman, he would likely have been shut out of the facility, and even if he had made his way in, he would have had a lonely lunch with his volunteers and the waitstaff. Reed, however, was given the opportunity to speak at a Bush-Cheney pastors' reception. A campaign aide stood by with a ledger asking pastors to promise to publicly endorse the president's reelection and host a "Citizenship Sunday" for voter registration and to identify people who would help organize a party for the president with other pastors.[3]

That day, Reed's aide collected 100 signatures from pastors who felt such actions were reasonable when liberals were closing in. Federal tax law prohibits intervening in elections, but what's a skirmish with the IRS when the fate of a nation is at stake?

Such thinking also inspired "Pulpit Freedom Sunday" in September of 2008, when Christian churches banded together to press the issue. About 20 miles from my home, a pastor in Bethlehem, Georgia, used that Sunday to tell his congregation that Christians must vote for Senator John McCain in the presidential election because he "holds more to a Biblical worldview."[4] Within a year, the pastor resigned his pulpit to run for Congress as a Republican candidate.

The Rev. Wiley Drake of First Southern Baptist Church in Buena Park, California, also participated in and defended the move: "According to my Bible and in my opinion, there is no way in the world a Christian can vote for Barack Hussein Obama. Mr. Obama is not standing up for anything that is tradition in America."[5]

The not-so-subtle inference was that God had a stake in this election, and we all knew who He was voting for.

Many people find such divisive partisanship among the faithful repulsive while others see it as confusing. People expect politicians to talk about politics. They anticipate that their speeches will be laden with legislative proposals and politically contingent visions for the future and a splash of mud to stain the opponent. But pastors banging pulpits in favor of tax cuts or government spending or specific social welfare programs as if the bill in Congress had been overnighted from the Almighty feels like an abuse of a sacred calling.

• • •

I often joke that I was "raised right." The phrase has a double meaning. I was blessed with two wonderful parents whose love was ever present and who attempted to instill in me uncommon principles such as discipline, generosity, respect for others, and a love for Jesus. I was also raised in a home that was, in Southern-speak, conservative as the day is long. As is true of most evangelical Christians, no one wondered what our election ballots looked like.

Conservative Christians aren't alone in this. The partisan "Christian Left" is often equally complicit. Though they hold the opposite positions on issues, the Christian Left's approach isn't much different from that of the Right. In fact, a 2010 study conducted by the Paul B. Henry Institute showed that while 44 percent of evangelical pastors said they had publicly supported a political candidate in the last election, 40 percent of (typically more liberal) mainline Protestant pastors said the same.[6]

The media have bemoaned how Religious Right leaders cozied up to President Reagan and both President Bushes. They've made much of how some Christians inferred that Bush was "the chosen one." The criticisms are, I think, fair ones. But when religious leaders on the left get their chance to hang out in the halls of power, they take it, too.

In 1996, President Clinton was in a vicious battle over the national budget. Fifteen prominent leaders from the progressive National Council of Churches traveled to Washington to meet with the president in the Oval Office. As the meeting closed, they "laid hands on him" and prayed that he would be "strong for the task" of opposing the Republican Congress.[7]

The legacy continues. Today, Derrick Harkins serves as both pastor of Nineteenth Street Baptist Church in Washington, D.C., and the faith outreach director for the Democratic National Convention.

Or consider left-leaning Christian leader Jim Wallis. An ordained minister in the American Baptist Church, he won't be found behind a pulpit on Sunday mornings. He gave the Democratic weekly radio address after the 2006 midterm elections and has written several books, including *God's Politics*.[8] Wallis has been accused of affixing Bible verses to Democratic talking points and is "an adviser to Democrats."[9] In the 2004 presidential election year, Wallis's magazine *Sojourners* published full-page ads in publications including the *New York Times* that read, "God is not Republican...or Democrat." But the message seemed to be "God is probably a Democrat."

In 2008, Christian writer Donald Miller, especially popular among young Christians, also jumped into the fray. Not only did he publicly endorse Barack Obama, but he campaigned for him. Touring with Obama's "Faith, Family, and Values Tour," Miller emceed discussion forums in key battleground states. He charged that Republican stands on economic issues are "Biblically suspect" and made a Christian case for voting for Barack Obama.[10]

When asked why a talented writer leveraged his influence in such a controversial way, he responded, "Religious leaders are very powerful, and Republicans cater to them and cannot win without the religious vote...but if you are asking if it was worth it to sell the church to the Republican Party, I would say no."[11]

I'd agree that Christians have often been the handmaidens of the Republican Party, but the response of many believers on the left has been to take the same misguided approach—just on the other side of the aisle. As Harvard professors Robert Putnam and David Campbell illustrate in their book *American Grace: How Religion Divides and Unites Us*, conservative Christians are often blamed for the conflation of religion and politics, but survey statistics show liberal congregations are the most politicized.

To be fair, most American Protestants are conservative evangelicals, and the sheer numbers of evangelicals make them easy targets. But many left-leaning Christians are sipping the same political Kool-Aid. Like the Church of England in the 1800s, which was frequently referred to as "the Tory party at prayer," the church in America is often reduced to the Republican or Democratic Party at prayer.

The religious Left remains dwarfed by the Right, however, in both number and influence. So the impact of their partisanship is minimal. But the Religious Right has become, in the words of a former speechwriter for George Bush, "the single most important constituency to the Republican Party."[12] For good or bad, Christians are viewed as partisans who are mostly aligned with conservative Republican politics.

* * *

Political parties don't run much risk in this deal. After all, the name of the political game is coalition building. When either the Religious Right or Left is merged with a particular party platform, those Christians can be courted, captured, and controlled. Democrats can then parade around the Religious Left in order to say, "See, some of us love Jesus, too," and call on them only when they need a spiritual counterbalance for a news story.[13] And the gargantuan religious presence among the Right can be used to give the impression that Republicans have cornered the God market.

I'm not sure most Christians have considered the cost of deep church involvement in partisan politics. Those on the right don't seem to wrestle with whether the Prince of Peace would unflinchingly support war or how following a God who cares about the poor would produce disciples who seem to blame the poor for their many woes (and ours). Those on the left are correct to highlight care for "the least of these" but often brush over the millions of aborted children who undoubtedly fall under that label.

Many on both sides lack a biblical framework for healthy engagement with the political process. Worse, few seem to consider the implications of their decisions. They know what might be accomplished by aligning their faith with a particular party, but they don't realize the price that must be paid, the sacrifices that must be made.

As a result, Christians allow the church—that wild and untamable "Body of Christ"—to be reduced to a voting bloc. We're like a teacher's union or senior citizens, a constituency that must be pandered to and pleased during campaign speeches so they'll cast their votes for a particular party. Politicians and inside-the-Beltway hucksters, come one, come all. The Christians are yours to be had.

Targeting Christian voters is not a recent phenomenon. When Grover Cleveland, the twenty-second and twenty-fourth president of the United States, said, "The Bible is good enough for me: just the old book under which I was brought up," he wasn't answering a reporter's question. He was expressing a sentiment that many Americans shared and making sure they knew he was a safe bet.[14]

Yet religious pandering has become more frequent in recent years as Christians have become more influential. Ronald Reagan, both Bushes, Bill Clinton, and Barack Obama have all used unmistakable biblical imagery to tip their hats to Christians. Other politicians at all levels of civil service do the same—they utilize religious language and imagery whether or not they hail from any Christian community or speak from a Christian worldview. Their words may seem harmless or coincidental, but many point out that these appeals are actually code language that the faithful recognize as their own.[15]

I'll never forget purchasing and reading George W. Bush's book *A Charge to Keep: My Journey to the White House* in 1999. My non-Christian friends thought the title sounded poetic, if not innocuous, but I recognized that the quotation was borrowed from Charles Wesley's wonderful old hymn "A Charge to Keep I Have." The first stanza reads,

> *A charge to keep I have,*
> *A God to glorify,*
> *A never-dying soul to save,*
> *And fit it for the sky.*

Neither the hymn nor the themes of this classic song are the subject of the book, but before I flipped to the first page, I felt like George Bush must be "one of us."

One might argue that these politicians are speaking from the faith chamber in their hearts when they use Christian references, that maybe we are cynical in judging their intentions. Several former Washington insiders would argue otherwise. David Kuo, the former second-in-command in President George W. Bush's faith office and special assistant to the president, claimed that Christians were often viewed by the administration as political pawns. In his book *Tempting Faith*, he wrote,

> National Christian leaders received hugs and smiles in person and then were dismissed behind their backs and described as "ridiculous," "out of control," and just plain "goofy." These leaders spent much time lauding the president, but were never shrewd enough...to wonder whether they were being used. They were.[16]

While many Christians believe that manipulating the political system achieves their own goals, the joke may be on us. Little progress has been made on the so-called Christian agenda during the last several decades, despite the election of many politicians who eloquently speak our language. And the mold of Christian-as-partisan-voter has cheated believers out of true engagement with the public square. The political Lucys place the culture-war footballs out around election time only to pull them back as the religious Charlie Browns come running.

When speculating on the question in electoral politics of "who is using whom," James Davison Hunter writes, "The obvious answer is to say that it is the candidates who cynically use the symbols of the culture war and thus one constituency or the other in the service of their own political ambitions."[17] Surely the church can do better.

. . .

Worse than being used by politicians, Christians diminish God by aligning Him with partisan preferences. Baptizing complex party platforms with religious vernacular makes our position synonymous with God's position. A simple legislative proposal, for instance, can be framed in such a way that a "true Christian" could not oppose it. Whether intended or not, dragging partisan politics into the sanctuary scribbles "thus saith the Lord" across opinions. Once the association is made, those on the other side of the aisle are not merely mistaken; they are apostate.

This language creates an unbiblical political litmus test for spiritual fidelity. Being a faithful Christian means voting a certain way or holding to certain political viewpoints. If one of the faithful falls out of line on the political end, his or her faith is called into question.[18] Some Christians speak as if denying certain policies is the equivalent of denying Christ. This also means that those who aren't of a particular partisan pedigree don't feel welcome in churches where Christians allow such associations. It communicates that Christianity "isn't for them." So Christian partisanship can actually become a hurdle to our efforts to share and spread the gospel.

Using politics as a measure of spiritual fidelity only strengthens the constituency and increases our worth as a voting bloc as many today find great value in faith's ability to moralize arguments and win debates.[19] This positive feedback mechanism keeps partisan faith humming along, but it can become a vortex in which a well-meaning believer can get lost.

Partisan thinking can also be irrational thinking. In the late 1980s, a majority of Democrats were convinced that inflation had risen under President Reagan, but in fact, it had fallen substantially. In 1996, most Republicans claimed that the deficit had increased under President Clinton, but in fact, it had shrunk steadily. Late in the Bush presidency, twice as many Republicans as Democrats believed the economy was performing well.[20] As one plunges deeper into the culture wars, one loses a sense of reality and embraces a partisan perception.

When people hear Christians speaking foolishly about political realities, should we not expect them to tune us out when we speak about the gospel? If they see the irrationality of Christian partisanship, how can they expect anyone to believe other incredible claims about God and Jesus?

Ross Douthat of the *New York Times* wrote, "Is there anything good to be said about the partisan mindset? On an individual level, no. It corrupts the intellect and poisons the wells of human sympathy. Honor belongs to the people who resist partisanship's pull, instead of rowing with it."[21]

While politicians don't risk much in the conflation of faith and party, the faithful place their integrity on the line. Christians like myself can't help wondering if this is Jesus' desire for His Body in the twenty-first century. Is the church to be reduced to a voting bloc, a constituency to be bought and sold? Are Christians to be seen as politicians in clerical collars? Such is the path of partisanship if Christians allow themselves to be led down it.

. . .

Today's faithful are growing intolerant of the sort of blatant partisanship that has marked the last several decades of Christian political engagement. I began sensing a change in 2007. I had been on assignment with several news outlets following Christian political engagement among those on the left and the right. I'd spoken with hundreds of Christians—pastors and activists, business leaders and teachers, college students and social entrepreneurs—whose words informed dozens of articles. What I saw and heard struck me.

Their stories were a lot like mine. Maybe they weren't raised in a staunchly conservative Christian household, but they'd grown up believing that those on the other side of the political aisle— even the Christian ones—were their enemies. They thought faithful Jesus-followers needed to jump feetfirst into the culture wars if they wanted to build the kingdom in a country that was slipping into moral decline. Having reflected further, their thinking shifted.

A few months prior to Hillary Clinton's conceding the Democratic presidential nomination to Barack Obama in June 2008, I'd penned a column for the *Atlanta Journal-Constitution* titled, "WWJD? Vote for Obama, More and More Young Evangelicals Say."[22] My thesis: this group of Christians voted Republican in high numbers, but their young people had grown disenchanted with the culture wars and were drawn to the language of "change" and "hope" flowing from the Obama campaign. If current trends persisted, they might cross party lines for the first time in their lives.

The column was based on two thoughts. I noticed a growing partisan schism among Christians through conversations with friends and interviewees, and I'd seen several polls that substantiated this sentiment. One such poll conducted by *Relevant* magazine—a publication influential among young Christians—asked, "Who would Jesus vote for?" The majority of respondents were self-described conservatives, and yet their top response was "Barack Obama."[23]

After the article was published, many expressed disbelief, if not horror, that people who called themselves "Christian" could pull the Obama lever. They were even more incensed that I would give this group a voice in a major publication and said I'd be hearing from them come November when I was proved wrong. The election came and went, and some exit polls indicated a notable shift among young Christians.[24]

I didn't hear from my detractors after the election, but they didn't seem to understand that this was not about Barack Obama or rising liberalism among young evangelical Christians. Rather, it pointed to a larger narrative about a whole generation of Christ-followers who believe the culture-war model is broken and want to liberate their faith from its partisan captivity. As they find and live out a faith of their own, they are no longer restricted to a single political party.

In 2001, the Pew Research Center for the People and the Press reported that 55 percent of white evangelicals ages 18 to 29 self-identified as Republican. Six years later, in 2007, only 40 percent did. Interestingly, the defected did not simply migrate to the Democratic Party. Most of them now consider themselves "independent" or "unaffiliated."[25]

As pastor and bestselling author Tim Keller says, today's Christians may be "the vanguard of some major new religious, social, and political arrangements that could make the older form of culture wars obsolete." He says, "After they wrestle with doubts and objections to Christianity many come out on the other side with an orthodox faith that doesn't fit the current categories of liberal Democrat or conservative Republican."[26]

When I lived in North Carolina, Elizabeth Dole was running for reelection to the United States Senate as a Republican. Democrat Kay Hagan opposed Dole. And though she was likeable, Hagan was still a Democrat. In a conservative state like North Carolina, party means far more than likeability. I assumed Senator Dole was a shoo-in.

Then Elizabeth Dole ran her infamous "godless ad." The 30-second commercial attempted to set up an association between Hagan and an atheist political action group that sponsored a fundraiser where she spoke, but the ad's claims went far beyond association.

"Godless Americans and Kay Hagan. She hid from cameras. Took godless money," the commercial's narrator said. "What does Kay Hagan promise in return?"

A female voice posing as Hagan answers the narrator's question: "There is no God."

Slipping in the polls, Dole decided to use the old tactic of insinuating that the Republican candidate loves Jesus and the Democratic candidate is a godless secularist who wants to chase God out of the public square. Dole's people didn't know that this worn-out tactic no longer resonated with conservatives or with Christians.

As it turned out, Democratic Hagan was an elder at First Presbyterian Church in Greensboro, where she taught Sunday School each week and was involved in youth mission trips. Liberal she might have been, but godless she was not.

North Carolinians were appalled, and many decided to stay away from polling centers on Election Day, even numbers of staunch Republicans. With one voice, the voters of this highly Christian and conservative state repudiated the religious and political game Dole was playing. Twenty years ago, those insinuations might have worked, but not now.

Dole plummeted in the polls, North Carolinians sent her packing, and the ordeal illustrates that change is afoot.

Many are growing so ill with the blurring of faith and partisan politics that they're abandoning the public square altogether. I can understand such exasperation, but I stress caution. Much good can be accomplished if Christians can learn to engage the political arena in a less partisan way.

Christians must be faithful not just within our churches, but throughout all spheres of life.[27] Good Christians are good citizens, and as such, they should establish a faithful presence in the public square as in media, business, science, education, and the arts. The question isn't, *"Should* Christians be involved in politics?"* but rather, *"How* should Christians engage politics?"*

Many prominent Christian figures in recent history have been terrible role models when it comes to partisan politics and their culture-war approach. Critiquing these leaders is helpful to a point, but we must also identify those whose lives demonstrate a better way. A few out there, I believe, set a better example with their public witness. One in particular comes to mind.

* * *

Growing up evangelical, I've always held Billy Graham in high regard. He's been able to navigate the booby-trapped maze of politics without losing sight of his calling or compromising his integrity. How did he make such an impact without plunging himself into partisanship or chasing power, without believing that politics was the answer to what's wrong with the world? I asked him during a visit to his home on March 31, 2011.

Dad was teaching a seminar at The Cove, Dr. Graham's training center nestled into the Blue Ridge Mountains of Asheville, North Carolina. He had met with the evangelist on several occasions during his life, but as Dr. Graham aged, his health wavered. Dad knew this might be the last chance he'd get to be with Dr. Graham in person. He arranged a visit to the evangelist's storied Montreat cabin, and brought me, my mom, and a pastor friend along.

The car followed a winding road until we arrived at a modest mountain home with a million-dollar view. The famous front porch was just how I'd imagined, adorned with worn rocking chairs and old flowerpots. I wondered which well-known figures had sat in those chairs.

Dr. Graham's aide instructed us to speak loudly and talk slowly before he led us inside.

Just inside the door and across from the kitchen, Dr. Graham sat in a small living room with a stacked stone fireplace. We each approached to shake his hand, but his kind eyes greeted us before his fingers could.

"It's such an honor to meet you," I said.

"No, no," he replied. "This is my honor. I'm so happy you took the time to stop by."

I could sense Dr. Graham's genuineness. He *was* happy we'd stopped by and he *was* honored by our visit.

A young lady dressed in nurse's scrubs brought a tray of iced tea as we circled Dr. Graham. We asked him questions about ministry, aging, his late wife, Ruth, and the time he had spent with various presidents. Eisenhower was the most spiritual president in his opinion, but he felt closest to Reagan, who, he said, still showed up in his dreams from time to time. Each time we asked a question, Dr. Graham shared a wonderful story. I felt like I was visiting my grandfather, if my grandfather were the greatest American evangelist who'd ever lived.

After listening to story after story for almost an hour, Dad invited me to ask Dr. Graham a question. I paused to take a sip of sweet tea before proceeding.

"Dr. Graham, you've been talking about your time with the presidents. I'm struck by the way you've been able to offer yourself as an encouragement, resource, and truth-teller to leaders from both parties," I said. "A lot of young people like myself today have witnessed how many Christian leaders got lost in the partisanship and the power that accompanies it. What advice could you offer to a new generation of Jesus-followers? How can we be more like you?"

Dr. Graham paused to gather his breath, his eyes searching the ceiling for the right answer.

"First, I'd say, don't try to be like me because I didn't always get it right," he said. "But also, with one exception, I never asked to meet with the presidents. They always asked to meet with me."

His words spoke volumes. When other Christians were jockeying for position or influence, Billy Graham focused on preaching the gospel. He rarely sought out politicians and refused many of the requests they made of him through the years.

His daughter, Gigi, chimed in:

> You know, Jonathan, I'd add something to that. I remember one time when Daddy took me to a dinner for everyone who had been on the cover of *Time* magazine. The Clintons were there even though they were going through a difficult time in their marriage. Daddy and I tried to be so gracious to them over dinner, but some people couldn't believe we'd do that because they didn't agree with the Clintons' politics. But Daddy always taught us that we are to love, the Holy Spirit convicts, and God judges. The problem is that some Christians try to do all three.

None will dispute that Billy Graham always tried to stay true to the advice he'd offered his daughter. You'd never find him on CNN excoriating a president or offering advice on tax policies. When Bill Clinton's impeachment scandal erupted in 1998 and most Christians were lobbing rhetorical bombs at the president, Dr. Graham came to his defense and preached forgiveness. He offered loving spiritual guidance while maintaining political neutrality. Bill Moyers once described Graham's political orientation by saying, "You know—both sides of the road."[28]

Almost one year before I met Dr. Graham, President Barack Obama had sat in the same room with him. Not much is known about what transpired in their 35-minute meeting except that they discussed their wives. Sources familiar with the conversation said the president shared "how lonely, demanding and humbling the office can be."[29] They prayed together before the meeting concluded.

I was with some conservative friends when the meeting was reported on television. "I can't believe he met with that guy," one person said. "I'd love five minutes with that socialist," another interjected. I'm sure many conservatives responded in like manner.

But the legendary preacher is no respecter of party. After his first meeting with Eisenhower, Dr. Graham remarked, "I didn't even know if he was a Democrat or a Republican."[30] President Obama was the twelfth occupant of the Oval Office to meet with Graham. In fact, every commander in chief since Harry Truman has sought out his advice and prayers. He read the Bible with Dwight Eisenhower, prayed with Gerald Ford, and is credited with the conversion of George W. Bush.[31]

Some conservative preachers I know couldn't enjoy such a generous and gracious meeting with a Democratic president. And many liberal Christians would have an equally difficult time had they been placed in a meeting with George W. Bush. Yet Graham possessed the uncanny ability to find commonality with those he might not always have agreed with.

When he was asked in 2007 why he never affiliated with Jerry Falwell's Moral Majority, Billy Graham replied,

> I'm all for morality, but morality goes beyond sex to human freedom and social justice. We as clergy know so very little to speak with authority on the Panama Canal or superiority of armaments. Evangelists cannot be closely identified with any

particular party or person. We have to stand in the middle in order to preach to all people, right and left. I haven't been faithful to my own advice in the past. I will be in the future.[32]

I long for more Christians to engage in the public square with the same integrity: resisting the pull of partisanship, standing courageously in the middle; speaking with love and mutual respect for those who claim other parties; clinging to the gospel, but not in a way that marginalizes listeners based on their political affiliations. Billy Graham is sought after as a source of wisdom and strength, not a constituency for pandering. Graham has effectively engaged in the public square, but none can claim him as their own. If only more Christians could do likewise.

As our car inched down the mountain road, slowed by the many switchbacks, I wasn't just inspired by Dr. Graham's genuineness, or the deep sense of love that emanated from the core of his being. I knew that in my short visit, I had brushed up against greatness. He challenged me with his advice, words he lived by. In some ways, my journey to Montreat had taken a lifetime, but encountering the evangelist's perspectives made the trip well worth the wait.

THREE

Christians at War

*A sick society must think much about politics, as a
sick man must think much about his digestion: to
ignore the subject may be fatal cowardice for the one
as for the other. But if either comes to regard it as the
natural food of the mind—if either forgets that we
think of such things only to be able to think of something else—then what was undertaken for the sake of
health has become itself a new and deadly disease.*

—C. S. LEWIS, "THE WEIGHT OF GLORY"

I was just leaving my dorm room on the morning of September
11, 2001, when the first plane hit. Most Americans say they
remember where they were and who they were with when they
learned of the attacks. The significance of the moment burned
the image into our memory like a cattle brand.

As I departed, I heard a friend shout down the hall: "A plane
has hit the World Trade Center." I rushed into his room just as
the replay tape rolled to show American Airlines Flight 11
smashing into the north tower of the World Trade Center,
between floors 93 and 99. My bag slid down my shoulder and
hit the floor as my body lowered to the couch.

The scene was gripping, worthy of a movie trailer for a summer blockbuster. Silence saturated the room as my friend and I continued to watch the smoke billowing out of the building. I wanted to say something, but overcome with disbelief, I couldn't get a word out. My vocal cords went on strike. I sat in silence, processing the horror.

I remained with my friend for the next several hours, watching more crashes and reports of terrorism roll in. As it did millions of other Americans, the news assaulted me with waves of intrigue, fear, and rage. The whole country needed therapy.

In the days that followed, emergency workers sorted through the rubble, and the Bush administration planned their response. The president, shaken and in need of counsel, invited almost three dozen religious leaders to join him at the White House for dialogue and advice. As the head of the Southern Baptist Convention, Dad was called to Washington.

Tim Goeglein, special assistant to the president and deputy director of the Office of Public Liaison, coordinated the meeting. Goeglein was a middleman between Bush and religious leaders and groups. The *Washington Post* called him "the pipeline to the President," whose job was to "keep the right happy."[1]

Charles Colson, a conservative Christian leader and former Nixon public liaison, once commented, "My experience has been a lot of times when we have had serious questions and we needed [Bush] administration backing to get them through... if we call Tim, all of a sudden things get through."[2]

During the days after 9/11, however, religious leaders had no problem getting through. The president felt he needed them close by.

As the group arrived, they were led through the tedious White House security checkpoint before being herded to the Eisenhower Building to draft a statement on how Americans should pray in a time such as this. A group of leaders who usually spend little time together found a common purpose. Tears and laughter were shared in a moment when both were needed. When their work concluded, the group relaxed and mingled. Tim Goeglein returned to pull Dad aside.

"James, the president would like to see you and a few others in the Oval Office," he said.

"I'll be happy to," Dad responded, trying to hide his elation.

A few moments later, six leaders were ushered to the room just outside the Oval Office. Those chosen included Dad, Franklin Graham, Roman Catholic cardinal Bernard Law, a Muslim imam, an Orthodox priest, and a Jewish rabbi. Nervousness reigned until the door swung open and President Bush's chief of staff, Andy Card, appeared.

"Gentlemen," he said. "The president will see you now."

Walking into the most famous office from sea to shining sea, each man shook the president's hand and took a seat. One by one, they pulled out their notes and began "advising" the president. Growing up, Dad always reminded us, "Even a fool is thought wise when he shuts his mouth." Thinking this was a good time to take his own advice, Dad sat quiet and attentive with the other guests in a semicircle around the president like an AA meeting for religious leaders. After much discussion, the president turned to him.

"James," he said. "You haven't said much. What do you think?"

"Mr. President, you and I are fellow believers in Jesus Christ," Dad said.

Bush nodded.

"We both believe there is a sovereign God in control of this universe."

The president nodded his head again.

"Since God knew that those planes would hit those towers before you and I were ever born, since God knew that you would be sitting in that chair before this world was ever created," Dad said, "I can only draw the conclusion that you are God's man for this hour."

At this, the president lowered his head and wept.[3]

On the same day, less than 200 miles southwest of the nation's capital in Lynchburg, Virginia, Jerry Falwell joined Pat Robertson via satellite on his *700 Club* telecast. His remarks during the show stand in stark contrast to the somber moment unfolding in the Oval Office:

> *Jerry Falwell:* And I agree totally with you that the Lord has protected us so wonderfully these 225 years. And

since 1812, this is the first time that we've been attacked on our soil and by far the worst results. And I fear, as Donald Rumsfeld, the Secretary of Defense, said yesterday, that this is only the beginning. And with biological warfare available to these monsters—the Husseins, the Bin Ladens, the Arafats—what we saw on Tuesday, as terrible as it is, could be miniscule if, in fact—if, in fact—God continues to lift the curtain and allow the enemies of America to give us probably what we deserve.

Pat Robertson: Jerry, that's my feeling. I think we've just seen the antechamber to terror. We haven't even begun to see what they can do to the major population.

Jerry Falwell: The ACLU's got to take a lot of blame for this.

Pat Robertson: Well, yes.

Jerry Falwell: And, I know that I'll hear from them for this. But, throwing God out successfully with the help of the federal court system, throwing God out of the public square, out of the schools. The abortionists have got to bear some burden for this because God will not be mocked. And when we destroy 40 million little innocent babies, we make God mad. I really believe that the pagans, and the abortionists, and the feminists, and the gays and the lesbians who are actively trying to make that an alternative lifestyle, the ACLU, People For the American Way—all of them who have tried to secularize America—I point the finger in their face and say "you helped this happen."

Pat Robertson: Well, I totally concur, and the problem is we have adopted that agenda at the highest levels of our government. And so we're responsible as a free society for what the top people do. And, the top people, of course, is the court system.

Jerry Falwell: Pat, did you notice yesterday the ACLU and all the Christ-haters, People For the American Way, NOW,

etc. were totally disregarded by the Democrats and the Republicans in both houses of Congress as they went out on the steps and called out to God in prayer and sang "God Bless America" and said "let the ACLU be hanged"? In other words, when the nation is on its knees, the only normal and natural and spiritual thing to do is what we ought to be doing all the time—calling upon God.
Pat Robertson: Amen.[4]

I stood in front of my television set when I heard Dr. Falwell's remarks. The same frustration, fear, and anger I had felt days earlier welled up inside me. *Is any sin worse than another in God's eyes? Is God really a petty Being, lurking in the shadows and tallying up sin, waiting to even the score? Is God especially angry at certain sinners—namely abortionists, gays, and members of the ACLU—and does He overlook the greed, lust, and violence rampant among the rest of us?*

My mind recalled a scene from the Gospel of John.[5] As Jesus walked with His disciples, they asked Him a fascinating question about a disabled beggar: "Rabbi, who sinned, this man or his parents, that he was born blind?"

Jesus turned to them and replied, "Neither this man nor his parents sinned, but this happened so that the works of God might be displayed in him."

Then Jesus gave the man his sight.

I don't know why God allowed 9/11 to happen. What I know about God leads me to believe that He didn't cause it, and it wasn't His way of settling some cosmic score with liberal Americans. I can only say for sure that it was an opportunity for God's power and presence to be made known, an occasion for us to place our trust in Him despite our grief and uncertainty so that He could bring healing.

The false thinking that suffering always results from sin more closely resembles the Hindu conception of Karma than the Christian God of the Bible.[6] No human can trace the locus of this tragedy to particular sins, and we shouldn't try.

Five days later, Dr. Falwell apologized for the comments:

> I do not know if the horrific events of September 11 are the judgment of God... but if they are, that judgment is on all of America—including me and all fellow sinners—and not on any particular group.[7]

His public statement communicated a thoughtfulness not always present in the culture wars. Such a moment of contrition should have been met with widespread absolution. But many felt they couldn't forgive a man who chose to kick Americans when they were down.[8] Over the years, Dr. Falwell became known for his strong, often outlandish rhetoric. His response in that moment illustrates how culture-warring Christians often speak with a sour tone and rely on ruthless tactics.

. . .

We live in the age of opinion. And with so many opinions bombarding us daily, often the most ridiculous, most inflammatory, most contentious perspectives rise to the top. As a result, the age of opinion has become the age of incivility.

A Public Agenda Research poll showed that almost 80 percent of Americans said lack of civility is a "serious national problem." More than 6 in 10 agreed that social behaviors were ruder than in the past. These trends are spurring a violent society and coddling a culture that produces road rage, sports fan rage, cell phone rage, and yes, even maniacs like Arizona gunman Jared Loughner.

Nowhere was this more apparent than during the health-care reform debates a few years ago when dissenters employed tactics that would make Aaron Burr wince. Senator Arlen Specter (D-Pa.) was booed for more than an hour and accused by one protestor of stuffing his pockets with lobbyists' money. The office of Representative David Scott (D-Ga.) was defaced with a four-foot swastika. In North Carolina a fistfight broke out at a town hall meeting hosted by Democratic Representative David Price. In Phoenix, more than a dozen protestors carried firearms outside the convention center where the president was speaking.

Rewind to November 2, 1822, when 79-year-old Thomas Jefferson sat down at his Monticello home in Virginia to pen these words: "The atmosphere of our country is unquestionably charged with a threatening cloud of fanaticism, lighter in some parts, but too heavy in all."[9] I'm amazed how little has changed in 190 years.

American culture today is plagued by a most distasteful disposition. For the past several decades, the American public square has grown divided and polarized. Angry tirades pollute our airwaves while name-calling and personal attacks saturate the halls of power. Simple issues that were once fertile ground for reasonable debates are now battlegrounds for bitter culture wars.

Christians gladly contribute to our current political climate. We struggle to shape public policy according to the amorphous standard of "Christian values." We fight against each other with unrivaled tenacity. Christians on the left villainize converts on the right as narrow-minded, antiquated, and uncompassionate. Christians on the right demonize believers on the left as unorthodox, compromising, and unpatriotic.

Such an acerbic environment led Mark Demoss of The Demoss Group to call for more respectful debate. A conservative publicist who has worked with Christian leaders from Chuck Colson to Franklin Graham, he partnered with liberal Lanny Davis in 2009 to launch the Civility Project. The statement they produced was a short pledge to be civil and fight incivility wherever it showed up. After its release, only three members of Congress agreed to sign the statement. The Civility Project was disbanded.

On MSNBC's *Countdown with Keith Olbermann*, Demoss shared a letter he'd received after the project was released. The respondent wrote,

> The gutless republicans do not need more gutless wonders like you in the rino party. You remind me of some one that would bring a rock or knife to a gun fight. The thugs, communists, racists, bigots, liars, Nazis, and American hating sons of b-tches in the democrat party are scum of the Earth and will do anything to win. I believe you have been watching too many old movies where the good guy [*sic*] always

win. Vince Lombardi put it best. Winning is not everything, it is the only thing.[10]

This is our world. One where winning is everything and the speech of many has become harsh, angry, judgmental, threatening, and confrontational. If a liberal doesn't like a conservative's position, he calls the conservative "stupid," "antiquated," or "bigoted." If a conservative doesn't like a liberal's position, he calls the liberal "elitist," "unpatriotic," or "anti-God." Opponents of affirmative action are "racists," pro-choice advocates are "baby-killers," and those who even question gay marriage are "homophobes." Conservatives are quick to compare modern events to Nazism and leaders to Hitler while liberals blame abortion clinic bombings on the pro-life movement.

In a public forum two years ago, I attempted to tackle a particular political issue that tends to rankle conservatives. My position wasn't uncommon among Christians, and prior to publication, I characterized it as "centrist." I made every effort to balance my perspective and felt I had communicated in a reasonable tone.

Others apparently disagreed. Emails flooded my inbox—some were unkind and others flat-out vicious. One email stood above the rest. A well-known professor of Christian ethics at one of America's most prominent evangelical seminaries wrote me a scathing note. I tried to respond with grace, but each email was met with a more condescending reply. I was forced to ask the professor to stop contacting me because we were "unable to maintain a civil, Christ-honoring relationship" despite my best attempts. If he continued to chide me, I told him, I would block his address. He persisted; I blocked him.

Asking a professor of Christian ethics to behave in a Christian manner is ironic, but many Christians fail to rise above the fray and speak with balanced wisdom. We've joined and even contributed to the culture of coarseness. As a result, 70 percent of non-Christians aged 16 to 29 say Christians are "insensitive to others."[11]

As a Christian, I sometimes feel like University of Southern California Trojans coach John McKay after his first year with the Tampa Bay Buccaneers. After a successful career coaching the USC Trojans, Coach McKay discovered winning wasn't as easy for him in the Sunshine State. After an 0–14 season, the press wanted answers.

"What do you think of the execution of your team?" a reporter asked.

McKay replied, "I'm all for it."

Christian leaders who claim to represent the larger movement often so thoroughly misrepresent the rest of us that many would cherish clearing the deck and starting from scratch. Today's Christians believe we all need to learn how to disagree without being disagreeable. To listen more and speak less and perhaps infuse our debates with a modicum of respect. Turning imperative debates into an episode of *The View* doesn't help anything.[12]

People crave a civil society for both personal and pragmatic reasons. Most of humanity feels the offense of harsh words even when they are directed at others. I disagreed often with President George W. Bush when he was in office, but I bristled when I heard Senator Harry Reid call him a "liar." I winced when Al Gore growled, "He betrayed this country" before a rally of Tennessee Democrats. Picking on someone for long enough—even if they deserve it—will make you seem a bully and your opponent a martyr.

A coarse culture is also an unproductive culture—especially in a democratic society whose engine runs on compromise and coalition building. When incivility reigns, progress is stymied and compromise is replaced by stalemate. Judiciousness is eminently practical in such a system. As *Washington Post* columnist Michael Gerson writes, "On the whole, people drawn to a cause like to feel that those representing the cause are both amiable and peaceable."[13]

Christians need a rapid infusion of what Peggy Noonan calls "patriotic grace," which is to say, "a grace that takes the long view, apprehends the moment we're in, comes up with ways of dealing with it, and eschews the politically cheap and manipulative."[14] Many of the folks I've spoken with want exactly that. They desire what John Murray Cuddihy called a "culture of civility."[15] They long for the day when the American public square will be a place of passionate but reasonable discussion—resembling the Greek agora more than the Roman Coliseum.[16]

* * *

In addition to our *sour tone*, Christians must confront the *brutal tactics* that often walk hand in hand with the culture wars. Freud said, "Humans are wolves to fellow humans," and culture warriors seem to be particularly adroit at destroying their prey. Entrenched in political ideology and armed with a political strategy, culture warriors make use of political tools to achieve political goals. In this mode, enemies are abundant and victory is paramount. A few years ago, I stumbled into a den of sleeping predators and almost lost my hide.

I became an environmentalist at a Southern Baptist Seminary. Few people on the planet can say that. I was sitting in a theology class listening to a lecture about the general revelation of God in nature and became bitterly convinced that I was contributing to the muffling of God's voice around me through my destructive lifestyle.[17] Over the next few months, I decided to reflect on my life's habits and make many personal changes. But I still wanted to do more.

I contacted a group of pastors, professors, and leaders in the Southern Baptist Convention to help me draft a statement expressing a biblical view of creation care. A few months later, we finished the final version and I began circulating it among denominational leaders for their support. To my surprise, the signatures poured in. People were overjoyed that others in the denomination were stepping out on this issue.

Then, the heads of the Ethics and Religious Liberties Commission (ERLC) found out. The ERLC is the public policy arm of the Southern Baptist Convention, with offices in Nashville and Washington, D.C. The entity functions as a lobbying group within the most conservative wing of the Christian Right, and they don't like other people stepping on their turf. I had contacted their office early in the drafting process but received no response.

Then my initiative began gaining steam, and in their reading, it threatened to give the impression that there was variance among Southern Baptists on environmental issues. I became a liability.

ERLC leaders prodded me to abandon the efforts, luring me with soft bribes and hard threats. They told me that if I turned the project over to them, they would rewrite it. In return, they would pay for the public release and open up doors for speaking engagements. When I rejected the offer, they said they were obligated to contact signatories and dismantle the effort themselves. With the precision of a five-star political machine, ERLC leaders began locating signatories and trying to convince them to remove their names. Falsehoods circulated about my "hidden agendas" and "political ties." Emails sent with the cadence of machine-gun fire became impossible to contain.

At the time, I was a second-year seminary student, unaware of the power and determination of the establishment. I never expected and wasn't equipped to combat the hornets from the nest I'd accidentally kicked. The breaking point came late one night when I was studying for exams. I received a call from one of my favorite professors, someone I admire. He informed me that ERLC leadership was offering me one last chance to turn over the initiative. If I decided to move forward, the full force of their opposition would fall on me. This included telling "the truth" about my effort to denominational leaders, many of whom I considered heroes. I was given 24 hours to consider their offer and decide.

I hung up the phone and wept. I was attempting to act on my convictions under the guidance of wise counsel, but I was being not so kindly shown the door. Peeking behind the curtain of the establishment church, I was shocked to discover a political machine that looked a lot more like Washington than Nashville. Rather than turn the initiative over to the group, I released it to the public. Major news media picked up on the story, and soon the toothpaste was out of the tube. The ERLC moved on, and I was left to ponder all that transpired.

Is this the current state of the Christian Church in America? Has Christ's Bride become so hungry for influence that she will stop at nothing to protect her power? Is this community at the point where seminary professors will threaten students at the beckoning of the establishment?

Sadly, yes.

I'm not the only one who has been the target of such tactics. I've met many over the years who've shared similar experiences. Like me, they deviated from the platform, called out someone on the home team, or failed to run their projects through the gatekeepers. They were ignored, ridiculed, or discredited and might as well have been handed the black spot from Robert Louis Stevenson's *Treasure Island*.

The political, economic, and social systems in our country don't exist to glorify God. They were built to turn a profit, grow an empire, consolidate power. Some Christian churches, leaders, and organizations have been co-opted by these systems with the promise of benefiting from the resources and power they produce. Experiences like mine serve as a warning to all who might challenge these human systems in which Christian entities are enmeshed. Don't expect to be embraced because you are a good person trying to accomplish a worthy goal or even because you're "right." Expecting culture warriors to leave you alone because you are a good person is like expecting a bull not to charge you because you are a vegetarian.

Cal Thomas and Ed Dobson, once high-level leaders in the Moral Majority, say they saw this kind of marginalization employed on people who stepped out of sync with the movement.

"Those who doubted or questioned our power were dismissed. Those who warned of danger were ignored, ridiculed, or condemned," they write.[18]

Ed Dobson admits that he was the victim of such treatment despite faithful service and conservative commitments. After leaving the Moral Majority, Dobson and several other religious leaders were invited to the White House to meet with President Bill Clinton. When interviewed by *Christianity Today*, he made some favorable comments about the president. Dobson later received a faxed copy of the article from Jerry Falwell. Across the margin, his former employer scribbled, "Unforgivable compromise. Don't ever call me again."[19]

Ousting is a typical culture-war tactic. We take someone who has different thoughts or convictions and declare them anathema. We cut them off. Then we chop off anyone who likes that person. Then anyone who likes the person who likes that person also has to be cleaved. The result is an insulated group in an isolated echo chamber where conservatives become more conservative and liberals become more liberal. No one has permission to think for themselves.

Such responses remind me of John 16:2, when Jesus says, "For you will be expelled from the synagogues, and the time is coming when those who kill you will think they are doing a holy service for God" (NLT).

Jesus' words instruct us. Some in the faith community will always believe that they've been commissioned by God to purify the church of all who think "differently." They will work to expel people from the community in the name of God, convinced that heaven looks on them with favor for their efforts.

What if Christians were known for listening before speaking, for seeking to understand before demanding to be understood? What if they were adept at facilitating dialogues rather than debates? What if we diverted energies to finding common ground with our Muslim and Hindu and Buddhist and atheist neighbors where we might work to accomplish good together? The air would literally be sucked out of many religious critics' sails.

Senator Alan Simpson spoke truth when he noted that if one travels the high road in Washington, one won't encounter much traffic.[20] In my own life, I want to tread the high road. I know the choice won't be easy and that, at times, I will stumble and fall. As angry as I want to be at those who've treated me harshly, I recognize that I'm one fork in the road away from the same path.

Apart from Christ, I could wake up tomorrow and become the very person I promise myself I will never be. So I must fix my eyes on this high road, and walk with humility and grace. The Scriptures exalt servitude, not strength. They instruct that the last shall be first. Living out the teachings of Jesus will not inspire us to rise to the top, but rather to stoop to the floor and wash the feet of others. And it's not just Jesus' life that instructs. On the cross we find Christ's greatest power exemplified in weakness. Perhaps there's a lesson there for us all.

FOUR

Our Constant Temptation

Whom the gods would destroy, they first make mad with power.

—EURIPIDES

My stomach grumbled in sync with my car's engine as I sat outside the headquarters of a prominent Christian advocacy group. They had invited me to speak to their advisory board about the changing landscape of young Christians. Thumbing through my notes, I wondered how they might receive my conclusions from the data I had compiled.

Like other conservative Christian organizations, they were reeling from Barack Obama's clobbering of Senator John McCain. A surprising number of young Christian voters had placed their confidence in the Democratic nominee, and much was being made of Christians' "broadening agenda." They scrambled to understand this demographic as they regrouped.

Data in hand, I entered a room full of conservative thinkers that included college and seminary professors, ethicists, pastors, and lobbyists. They greeted me with warm smiles, but their spotlight stares pierced the silence.

"I want to thank Jonathan for joining us today to present on what he sees happening among American Christians," the organization's president said. "I haven't always agreed with his perspective, and I know some of you haven't either. At the same time, he's done his homework, so I asked him to join us. Let's make him feel welcome."

The skeptical crowd gave me tepid applause, which sounded like a cross between a poetry reading and the golf channel.

I grabbed my notes and approached the lectern.

"A shift, a stirring is happening among the faithful," I said. "Some have called it a seismic shift while others called it a minor change. Rising Christians believe, think, and are engaging politics differently than many in the last generation. They are tired of the partisanship, weary of the warring, and ready for a less divisive expression of what it means to follow Jesus in the twenty-first century."

Measuring my breaths, I talked about young people's perception that the Christian Church and its leaders had become intoxicated with power. In the last several decades especially, I argued, we've fought for a seat at the world's mightiest table. Yet, many are wondering if it was worth the cost.

"Power, like a tractor beam, pulls one in whether or not one wants to go," I said. "If this organization wants to be successful in penetrating the minds of a new generation, it must be willing to say 'no' to chasing clout and 'yes' to following the Jesus of the Bible. This Jesus was uninterested in acquiring earthly power, and infatuated with pursuing the powerless."

Brows lowered, throats cleared, and chins raised. I could tell this was going to be a tough crowd. But even if this consortium of culture warriors wasn't ready to accept the new reality, they all recognized that the gears of change were beginning to move. Like many others, they needed to understand the current shift if they wanted to survive.

. . .

The thirst for political power has threatened the faith for most of Christian history, but not all of it. The earliest Christians in Rome refused to get entangled in partisan politics. They did not accept public office, opted out of any governing responsibilities, and avoided serving in the military. First-century believers were so removed from the divisive political atmosphere in Rome that the philosopher Celsus accused them of trying to "privatize" religion.[1]

But Christians were not totally disengaged from politics. A study of the first generations of Christians is a lesson in how to engage the public square without forgetting the gospel or drowning in political power. This growing group of Jesus-followers made great strides on issues such as infanticide, slavery, and an early expression of women's rights.[2]

They knew that politics is not the true threat; it's thirst for power. Power can shipwreck even the most faithful follower. This approach to politics changed, however, in the fourth century when the Roman emperor Constantine "converted" to Christianity. He handed the faithful an incredible amount of influence, appointing bishops to high-ranking public office and exempting clergy from paying taxes. When the Roman army marched, their shields bore "the mark of Christ." "Christendom" was born, and the newborn babe's hungry cries for power echoed throughout the world.

The church soon left the underground and began constructing buildings with land and subsidies provided by the state. In return for the empire's "kindness," bishops allowed the "Christian monarch" to help settle doctrinal controversies and influence church councils. Prior to this period, the church had largely remained neutral in political affairs, but now it began taking sides. The church's success was linked to the empire's success, and "preservation of the empire became the decisive criterion for ethical behavior."[3]

A movement that had once centered on the teachings of Jesus and caring for the vulnerable now sat at the world's most powerful table. Less than 500 years after Jesus declared God's kingdom, early Christians were already abandoning it in pursuit of an earthly empire. As Søren Kierkegaard said, "Christendom has done away with Christianity without being quite aware of it."[4]

The enduring legacy of this paradigm shift among the faithful is so significant that when *Time* magazine recently released its "100 Events That Changed the World," Constantine's reshaping of Christianity fell just behind "Jesus Christ Founds New Religion." Many critics of contemporary Christianity, in searching for the origin of our current problems, end up pointing a finger at Constantine. But simply blaming Christendom fails to get to the sin behind the sin, which is the innate human thirst for influence, power, and supremacy.

I felt power's pull a few years ago when I received an email with a subject line screaming, "The Opportunity of a Lifetime." No, it wasn't an offer from a Nigerian prince donating me a portion of his wealth or a typo-laden letter from a supposed attorney awarding me an heirless inheritance. A prominent, nonpartisan Washington think tank was putting together a broad coalition of religious leaders to support common-ground agendas on divisive issues.

They invited me to sign on to the effort and come to Washington, D.C., as part of a select group to be featured at the press conference. Having read their position paper and finding it agreeable, I responded that I'd be happy to join them.

At the release, my heart thumped as I read my statement and gave the rationale for supporting these positions. Members of the press shot back questions to cross-examine each of us, and we had to think fast. After the press conference, we were chauffeured to the Capitol Building, where we met with congressional leaders to share our ideas with them. The schedule was furious, and the day raced by like a school of minnows.

After I returned home that evening, I couldn't contain my smile as I peeled back the sheets and slipped into bed. I recounted all of the day's amazing events: standing alongside far more accomplished leaders to field questions from journalists, staring at the dentil molding and worn floors in the Capitol and knowing that I was standing in the same place where heroes once stood. I'd been trying to downplay my elation all day, but I was a carnival of adrenaline.

I've arrived, I thought, grinning into the darkness. *Important people relish my thoughts. They want to hear my opinion. They've offered* me *a place of influence.*

Suddenly, I was aware that the hook of power had caught me in the mouth and was reeling me in. My day had begun with feelings of inadequacy and undeservedness but had morphed into a love affair with power and position. My puffed-up chest fell like a spent balloon.

A few weeks later, I met with a mentor—an older, wiser gentleman who was also part of the effort in Washington. Unlike me, he deserved the invitation and added prestige to the signatory list. As I placed my latte atop the coffee shop table and faced him, he noticed the consternation on my face.

"Jonathan, I was very proud of the stand you took on these issues. It required much courage. But I need to warn you of something."

I peered over my mug pretending I didn't already know what he was about to say.

"Beware of the power."

He paused.

"Beware of the seduction."

He paused again.

"I've been in this work a long time, and when I returned home, I felt far too comfortable with the whole affair. As faithful Christians, we may be compelled to enter the political arena from time to time. But we should always be uncomfortable there."

I wondered if he'd been reading my journal or my mind or eavesdropping on my prayers. He seemed to know exactly what I'd been struggling with.

"Too many Christians who have come before us have walked through the halls of power and lost themselves," he reflected, staring out the window. "Never forget the lessons they teach us."

Every good mentor wields the lance of gentle truth, and his pricked my heart. I felt undressed by my own desire to be more and do more and achieve more. I became empathetic to all the Christian leaders who've rushed fast and hard into partisan politics during my lifetime. I realized how easy it was to swoon over a seat at the table and march to the commands of modern-day Constantines.

*   *   *

As I shared this story from the lectern during my talk for the Christian advocacy group, I felt the mood in the room begin to shift from curiosity to animosity. I wanted the audience to know that what I experienced was more than the faint reverberations of power's deception, that it was a temptation inside us all. The lust for power has plagued followers of Jesus since our faith's inception, and it's alive and well in all of our hearts. I began telling them a story they all knew well—the tale of Christianity in modern-day "God-blessed America."

America favored Christian people and principles throughout the first half of the twentieth century. In fact, until the latter part of the century, America might have been generously described as a "Christian society." During the 1920s, for example, Christians responded to our country's drinking problem by mobilizing in support of Prohibition and passed legislation that would be laughable today.[5]

Prohibition did not last, but Christian influence did. After World War II concluded, America experienced a spiritual revival of sorts.

I recently asked my 90-year-old grandmother what her favorite decade was. She said, "I liked growing up in the '30s and I liked the '50s pretty well too." When asked what about the 1950s stuck out to her, she said, "People knew what was right then, and they did it. We didn't have the crime and everything we have today. Most young people respected their elders and went to church on Sundays 'cause we knew it was the right thing to do."

Weekly church attendance in the 1950s soared to new highs—from 37 percent in 1950 to 51 percent in 1957.[6] If you wanted to run for a public office in America, regular attendance was pretty much a prerequisite. Gospel tunes mixed with popular music on mainstream radio stations, Christian arguments and ideas were persuasive, and people maintained great respect for clergy and the institutional church.

But the religiosity Americans were experiencing was different from the faith of early Christians. The revival of the 1950s has been called "the high tide of *civil* religion"[7] and might perhaps be described as a loose commitment to a convenient cultural faith. When asked, "Why do you go to church?" in a public survey during that decade, most Americans responded, "The need or desire for some sort of inspiration or uplift."[8]

So undistinguished was the religious fervor in the mid-twentieth century that President Dwight Eisenhower proclaimed, "Our government makes no sense unless it is founded on a deeply felt religious faith—and I don't care what it is."[9]

One critic responded, "President Eisenhower, like many Americans, is a very fervent believer in a very vague religion."[10]

It was as if many Americans who showed up at the post-war party were blindfolded, spun around, struck the Christian piñata, and stayed around to eat the candy. Regardless, Christian muscles were fully flexing throughout the public square at the time. The phrase "In God We Trust" was named the country's official motto and "under God" was inserted into the pledge of allegiance. But this time of Christian dominance did not last.

Harvard University's Robert Putnam and David Campbell describe the American experience over the last five decades as "a shock and two aftershocks." The shock came with the revolution of the 1960s and '70s, which brought a blitzkrieg of cultural change to America. It was as if everything many of her citizens held dear had been placed in a bottle, shaken up, and spewed out.

Politically, the shock came in a wave of "movements" that began pushing America toward pluralism, inclusiveness, and, in some cases, secularism. Courageous African American leaders forced America to confront her racism as they marched in the civil rights movement. A blood-soaked Vietnam brought on a fierce anti-war movement. A growing awareness of ecological degradation awakened the environmental movement. And changing sexual standards throughout society made possible the gay rights and women's rights movements.

The courts also seemed to unravel other edges of America's cultural fabric. *Engel v. Vitale* banned state-sponsored prayer in schools in 1962, *Abington v. Schempp* banned mandatory Bible reading in 1963, *Griswold v. Connecticut* legalized contraception in 1965, and *Roe v. Wade* legalized abortion in 1973.

Socially, our nation underwent an unprecedented metamorphosis. Illegal drug use grew as marijuana and LSD achieved the status of chic, feminism and women's liberationists fought to redefine gender roles, and "Hollywood" began increasing the amount of profanity and promiscuity in movies and television shows.

Religiously, the creeping liberalism of the earlier part of the century was threatening traditional orthodox theology. By the 1960s, the growing religiosity of many Americans had developed the tumor of skepticism. The academy fully embraced biblical criticism and moral relativism and slaughtered sacred cows from the authority of Scripture to the plausibility of miracles. The number of Americans claiming religion was "very important" fell from 75 percent in 1952 to 52 percent in 1978, and weekly church attendance plummeted.[11]

I remember my dad telling me stories when I was growing up about his experiences in the 1970s at the Southern Baptist Theological Seminary. At the time, Southern had grown theologically liberal like many other institutions of higher learning. Christians with traditional biblical theology were rattled, shaken, or transformed from the moment they stepped onto campus.

Dad was an eager mind from a rural town in Georgia called Oakwood. Like many students, he walked onto campus with a more conservative theology and a strong sense of calling to Christian ministry, but was met with hostility from enlightened academics. Professors prayed to their "heavenly mother," poked fun at students who desired to share their faith with non-Christians, and scoffed at the idea that Jesus Christ was resurrected as the Bible claims.

"The right and responsibility to live out my beliefs was under tremendous attack, even among those who claimed to also be Christian," Dad reminded me. "I felt like I was under oppression my entire seminary career."

What Dad was experiencing in seminary, others were experiencing in the marketplace and public square. Religious people and leaders believed their principles, convictions, and worldviews were being threatened on all fronts. They believed our country was, in the words of Robert Bork, slouching toward Gomorrah. Many felt they were now being faced with a choice: resist or be relegated to cultural obscurity.

*   *   *

When the American cultural revolution swept our nation, *liberal* Christians had been engaged in partisan politics for some time. Influenced by what Christian theologian Walter Rauschenbusch and others termed "the social gospel," they openly rallied behind more progressive causes and the politicians who supported them. The much larger faction of conservative Christians, however, did not have a unified political presence during the early twentieth century. They had no need to enter the public square; it distracted them from what they believed was the church's true work of evangelism. But they now felt assaulted. Like a cornered cat, conservatives leapt out with claws extended.

"The question was no longer whether you could make a case for political involvement," says Michael Cromartie, director of the Evangelical Studies Project at the Ethics and Public Policy Center in Washington, D.C. "The issue became which side you were on."[12]

Pastors began preaching about "moral decay." Christian mobilization efforts—from the Christian Coalition to the Moral Majority to Concerned Women for America—were formed to fight against political liberalism and influence national elections. These groups began educating Christians on political issues, encouraging them to get involved in the political process and vote for the candidates who most supported "Christian" positions. The fuse of the modern culture wars was lit, and Christians everywhere were marching to "take back America for Christ."

The tragic side effect of enlisting in the culture wars was that the Christian mission in the United States was now being reframed in terms of conflict. Believers expressed themselves "almost exclusively in the language of loss, disappointment, anger, antipathy, resentment and desire for conquest."[13] Some Christians began singing an ever-repeating loop of the old Groucho Marx tune, "Whatever It Is, I'm Against It." This legacy continues today.

The business of opposition is to oppose; that now seems to be all some Christians do. They've rewritten the story of Jesus' reinstatement of Peter in John 21:15. Here Jesus asks His disciple three times if he loves Him. When Peter replies "yes," Jesus asks him to feed and tend His sheep. Jesus doesn't ask him to picket the wolves. The mark of followship is defined in positive, not negative, terms. But some Christians seem to focus more on what they fight *against* rather than what they fight *for*.

A book I recently stumbled across, *The Gospel According to the New York Times*, illustrates this mindset and employs typical culture-war tactics. The author first explains the abhorrent values that the *Times* represents and then conjures up fear by showing how the newspaper intends to destroy Christians' values and way of life: "The most powerful news organization on earth, *The New York Times*, employs a highly versatile array of journalistic devices to mold the American mind and draw the lightly committed and unwary into the paper's web of beliefs and values."[14]

These mechanisms comprise what the author refers to as "culture creep," and the only way for a patriotic, God-fearing Christian to respond is to wage war. Readers are urged to:

- "learn to identify and combat culture creep,"
- "expose conflicts of interest involving the *Times*,"
- "devise an effective system of apologetics that will enable your belief system to prevail in disputes with those who follow the *Times*' gospel,"
- "establish an opposing news organization."

But perhaps the most honest and humorous suggestion given is to "take over the *Times*." No joke. The author is suggesting that readers cease whatever they are doing to conquer one of the world's largest newspapers.

How should they do this? The author includes a strategy for stockpiling "a huge war chest" of financial resources and turning minority stockholders against the organization's parent company. If that doesn't work, minority shareholders need to take advantage of the legal system and "harass and snipe away at the parent organization and its worldview through lawsuits."

The Gospel According to the New York Times was released by the publishing arm of the Southern Baptist Convention and is the kind of messaging that makes the Christian movement appear to be a disgruntled cohort of reactive naysayers trying to take control of the world.

By the 1990s, when this was published, Americans—both religious and non-religious—had caught a full glimpse of power-hungry Christians, and not everyone liked what they saw. Many Christians began abandoning the most partisan Christian efforts. During this time, Jerry Falwell's Moral Majority was dissolved and church attendance was again slipping. According to Robert Putnam and David Campbell, many became "increasingly uneasy about mixing religion and politics"[15] and "unhappy about the growing public presence of conservative Christians."[16]

* * *

The 1990s ushered in a golden era for America in many ways. Other than the short Gulf War and a few minor skirmishes, our nation remained relatively at peace. The threat of communism and nuclear war subsided, the stock market soared, and many were achieving the iconic American dream.

But society was not quite as stable as purported. American stomachs began turning due in part to the overly politicized

Christian Church, which now felt angry, reactionary, and triumphalistic. From the 1990s until the present day, we've been rumbling through the "second aftershock," a backlash against the backlash. The church is now feeling the vibrations of this period in at least two ways.

The church is *hemorrhaging from the inside.* As Christian involvement in the culture wars swelled over the last several decades, regular church attendance slouched—interrupted briefly during the months following the 9/11 attacks. Why are they leaving? According to a Gallup Poll, when Americans were asked to explain the decline in religious observance that they were seeing around them, one of the most frequent replies was the church was too involved with current social and political battles.[17]

Having come of age during the first aftershock period, young people today seem especially dissatisfied. A culture-warring church is the only one they've experienced, and they are running away as fast as they can.

A 2010 headline on the front page of *USA Today* warned, "Young Adults Less Devoted to Faith," and they weren't kidding.[18] According to LifeWay Research, two-thirds of young Protestants between the ages of 18 and 22 leave the Christian Church.[19]

Such statistics led Thom and Sam Rainer in their book *Essential Church* to write, "The American church is dying...Not only are we losing our nation to the ways of the world, but we are not winning our own children in Christian families. Multitudes are dropping out of church." Thirty-one percent fewer young people regularly attend church today than in the heat of the American cultural revolution.[20]

The church is also *repelling people from the outside.* The perceptions of non-believers about Christians in America have soured like unrefrigerated milk. Aware of the shifting landscape, pollster Dave Kinnaman and culture watcher Gabe Lyons investigated these perceptions in 2007. Among young non-Christians who've only witnessed the manifestation of Christianity during the first aftershock, only 16 percent said they had a "good impression" of Christianity. When narrowed to "evangelical Christianity," only 3 percent said the same.

The reasons behind these sentiments, according to Kinnaman and Lyons, are that non-Christians disapprove of our "entrenched thinking...empire-building...[and] us-versus-them mentality."[21] They dislike Christians' "swagger," the way they always seem to be in "attack mode," and the perception that they are "overly motivated by a political agenda."[22] Ninety-one percent said they perceived Christians as "anti-gay," 70 percent as "insensitive to others," 87 percent as "judgmental," and 75 percent as "too involved in politics."[23]

"In studying thousands of outsiders' impressions, it is clear that Christians are primarily perceived for what they stand against," Kinnaman and Lyons concluded. *"We have become famous for what we oppose, rather than who we're for."*[24]

In short, people seem to be reacting not against the church itself, but in part against the culture-war mentality that pervades the church. Many in the church spent the last several decades lashing out against the culture; now culture is returning the favor. Not coincidentally, the church is withering in the United States by almost every data point. Church attendance is declining, Christianity's cultural influence is fading, and many young people are finding places outside the church where they can express their spirituality without the baggage. Americans are saturating the church with their absence.

Those inside the church don't want to stay, and those outside the church don't want to start. These trends combine to weaken Christians' influence in society as a whole.[25] Christian faith is moving from ubiquity to the margins in America—from dominance to cultural irrelevance.

"While we remain decisively shaped by religious faith," wrote Jon Meacham of *Newsweek* in 2009, "our politics and our culture are, in the main, less influenced by movement and arguments of an explicitly Christian character than they were even five years ago."[26]

Americans will always struggle with each other, but Christians as a group are quickly losing the cultural cachet to contend as they once did. With each new year, the Christian movement in America seems less consequential. So the culture wars of tomorrow will not look like those of yesterday that were dominated and incited by Christian leaders and interest groups. Such a shift underscores one of the greatest reasons today's Christians are abandoning the culture wars: the fight itself is effectively over.

*   *   *

I paused to allow the audience at the prominent Christian advocacy group to reflect on what I was saying.

"We're a part of a larger story," I said. "It's a story of a faith that felt the culture coming apart at the moral seams and mobilized to mend it. But in our frenzied effort to recover the past, I wonder if we've lost sight of the goal: Jesus Himself."

Brandon, a 32-year-old who has left the church, exemplifies the cultural shift that's taken place.

"Twenty years ago when I was looking at evangelical Christianity from the inside, it seemed like a movement bursting with energy to spread good news to people," he says. "Looking at it from the outside today, the message seems to have been lost in exchange for an aggressive political agenda."[27]

Over the last three years, I've interviewed dozens of young people who have defected. I always make sure to ask them why they left the church and what might make them consider returning. The word that has consistently emerged is "authenticity." They *do* want to follow Jesus, and they *do* want to be a part of the church. But they want a faith community that is free of agendas. Today's Christians encounter the Jesus of the New Testament—the One who emptied Himself to dwell among us—and they find Him calling us away from the pursuit of power to a life that looks more like the one He lived.

As Tony Campolo has said, "All too frequently, Christian activists at both ends of the spectrum see power as the primary instrument for saving the world. 'If we just had the power,' they say, 'we could set everything right.' I want to say to them, 'I wonder why Jesus didn't think of that!' "[28]

When the Roman prefect Pontius Pilate asked Jesus if He was the "king of the Jews,"[29] it was his way of saying, "Do I need to be worried about you? Is your kingdom going to threaten my kingdom?"

Jesus runs an end around: "My kingdom is not of this world. If it were, my servants would fight to prevent my arrest by the Jewish leaders. But my kingdom is from another place."[30]

Jesus' kingdom is otherworldly, totally new, and it will not be realized through the power or victories of armies and legislation. Like any kingdom, God's kingdom will only be established by increasing the reign of the King through expanding the number of subjects who are unrelenting in their commitment to Him.[31]

When Christians recognize that Jesus' kingdom is not of this world, they remember that they don't struggle against flesh and blood. Our enemies are not pornographers, humanists, socialists, religious extremists, racists, or even terrorists. Christians must grapple against spiritual and institutional powers, powers without a face at which to point our fingers and say, "You helped this happen."

If Jesus' kingdom were of this world, He told Pilate, then His followers would be playing by the world's rules. They would mirror the world's tone in their speech and employ the world's tactics to foster a physical uprising. But Jesus and His disciples looked nothing like this.

When the religious leaders attempted to make Jesus choose sides, He declined.[32] When one of His disciples attempted to employ the world's tactics at His arrest, Jesus rebuked him and displayed a radically different approach.[33] Through His life and ministry, Christ made it clear that His kingdom could not be pursued by marginalizing those who seek to marginalize you, attacking those who attack you, or combating "anti-Christian" earthly kingdoms by installing "semi-Christian" earthly kingdoms. Instead, Jesus calls His subjects to begin "loving, serving, and hopefully transforming the enemy who seeks to destroy you."[34]

When Methodist missionary E. Stanley Jones visited the Soviet Union at the height of its prominence, he was impacted by the citizens' devotion to their country and the Communist Party: "They're building their society, and they seem unstoppable, but their kingdom is built on force. I belong to a kingdom built on faith. Their foundation is shakable. The foundation of God's kingdom is unshakeable."[35]

A few years later in 1972, Jones penned *The Unshakeable Kingdom and the Unchanging Person*, in which he brazenly predicted the imminent fall of Communism and called on Christians to reinvest their devotion to something greater than party or country: the "unchanging person" of Jesus Christ. Rather than building His kingdom by force or coercion, Jesus used the bricks and mortar of love. Instead of hanging His hopes and dreams on the course of a country, He hung it all on a cross.

When one stands before Jesus on the cross, the kingdom is unveiled in its entire splendor and our modern understanding of social engagement is turned on its head. The kingdom, Jesus demonstrates, can never be won through a culture war because it promotes serving above winning, sacrifice above entitlement, giving above taking over.

As I turned over the last page of notes and decided to answer any questions, a hand shot up on my right flank.

"I'm convinced by your data and analysis," he said. "So what can we do as an organization to make some changes? We clearly need to begin reaching out to a new generation of Christians. How do you think we can begin working not only to understand them, but to address their concerns?"

Before I could answer, the president of the organization jumped in.

"We're already past our allotted time," he said. "So let's thank Jonathan for making the trip up here and sharing his opinions on this topic with us."

Awkwardness filled the room as he continued.

"I can tell you, Jonathan, from my perspective this is not unusual. Every new generation tends to be a little rebellious and a bit more progressive than the last," he said as if to pat me on the head. "But I'll tell you what I believe will happen. I believe this group of Christians will get a little older and come to realize what's at stake. They'll come to realize how important our work is. And when they do, they'll come to their senses and return home."

I squeezed out a courtesy smile, realizing that no amount of data, argument, or analysis could persuade him to rethink their culture-war agenda. Like many other culture warriors, he and his organization were too deeply invested. Their funders expected progress, politicians needed support statements, legislation needed lobbying. The power brokers in Washington had become their singing sirens, and this organization was hypnotized by their melodies.

• • •

I've encountered such a disposition among many battle-worn culture warriors, which I've come to call the "Hezekiah syndrome." King Hezekiah was the fourteenth king of Judah, and a well-intentioned, righteous man. During his reign, he was able to enact reforms to preserve the worship of God in the temple in Jerusalem and lead the people back to the laws of the Lord. But as happens with many who experience great power, pride set in.

In the book of 2 Kings, Hezekiah is visited by the envoy of a Babylonian prince. Flattered by the great empire's gesture, Hezekiah gives them the VIP tour. No place in his kingdom was off-limits. Hezekiah shows the Babylonians his palace and armory and the storehouses where all of Israel's gold, silver, and treasures are kept. Basking in his great accomplishments, Hezekiah foolishly educates the enemy.

After the king bids the foreign potentate adieu, the prophet Isaiah visits.

"Who were those men and what did they see?" the prophet asks the king.

"That was the prince of the most powerful nation on earth," Hezekiah replies. "He wanted to admire all we've amassed, so I showed him everything. I gave him a grand tour of all our treasures."[36]

Exasperated, Isaiah does what prophets do best: he prophesies. The time will come, he says, when every jewel, coin, and treasure in Hezekiah's palace will be carried off to Babylon. The country that so easily stroked his ego will destroy his empire. Even some of Hezekiah's own descendants will be taken away and become slaves in the palace of the Babylonian king.[37]

The prophecy is devastating. Hezekiah has just been told that all he has built, all the reforms he has enacted, the dynasty he has spent his lifetime constructing will be swept away by a foreign invader. The most important treasure a king has—his legacy—is now in jeopardy. Yet Hezekiah responds with shocking words:

"The message you have given me from the LORD is good." For he is thinking, "At least there will be peace and security during my lifetime."[38]

The story of this king speaks to us about the seduction of power. Hezekiah knew he could hold on to the kingdom for his lifetime, even though the downfall of his dynasty was impending.

I'm worried that many well-meaning Christian leaders today in positions of power are sitting in a seat similar to Hezekiah's and responding in the same way. They've sat upon the couch cushions of presidents and tasted the cuisine of state dinners. A mindset of self-preservation has set in. Long-term visions give way to short-term goals and compromise squelches integrity. When one has fallen prey to the Hezekiah Principle, even news of the impending destruction of everything one has worked for cannot induce a change. Nothing matters but momentary security. They've grown comfortable in the halls of power. But the jig is up.

Their efforts to recover the past have produced a bleak future for the church. Our churches are bleeding, and the public's negative perceptions about our faith chase away potential converts. And as these leaders are faced with a new generation that wants to shake off the seduction of ascendency, they don't know how to respond. In their minds, the cost of change is too great.

But history has no rewind button; it only moves forward. Change is coming.

As Eric Hoffer once said, "In times of profound change, the learners inherit the earth, while the learned find themselves beautifully equipped to deal with a world that no longer exists."[39]

Today's Christians are rising up to rediscover the faith in a world that is, not a world that was. They desire to reclaim the faith from the partisan spirit so pervasive among some Christians in America. Today's Christians want to avoid the most detrimental downfalls of the last generation. Rather than viewing others as political enemies to destroy, they are attempting to live out their faith in all areas of life and pursue a kingdom that is so vast and comprehensive that Washington could never hope to contain it. These Christians aren't consumed with a platform or a party or a policy; they are devoted to a person who emptied Himself to rule supreme over a new kind of kingdom.

FIVE

A Symphony of Voices

Things do not change; we change.
                    —HENRY DAVID THOREAU

As a child, one of my prized possessions was a Bible given to me by my parents. It was wrapped in cheap navy blue bonded leather, and my name was stamped on the cover in gold letters. Over the years, the gold letters faded and the bonded leather peeled at the corners, revealing itself as neither bonded nor leather, but I still treasured that book. This Living Bible translation, written in more colloquial English, was a welcome alternative to the KJV for a 12-year-old.

Over the years, it began to resemble a day planner. Raggedy church bulletins stuck out from between pages, underlined verses mapped the interior, and the initials of people who stabbed me in the back were scribbled in the margins next to imprecatory prayers and condemning passages.

I loved that book, but I wished it weren't so long. Pages as thin as a cell wall with seven-point font arranged into double columns. If God is so smart, I wondered, couldn't He condense what He wanted to say into a couple of chapters, or even better, a pamphlet? Why couldn't God be more economical with His words?

During the holidays, my father bribed us to read through the entire Bible during the upcoming year. "If you stick with it for the whole year, I'll give you each $100," he'd say. Looking down at the worn blue cover, I remember thinking, *You don't make enough money. This book is as thick as my femur!*

I now see the Bible's depth and breadth as a gift. It's unplumbable, with a word for nearly every life stage and conundrum humanity faces. The Christian Scriptures are as useful, as insightful, as revelatory to a modern businesswoman as to a medieval peasant or second-century Roman aristocrat. Only the Deity could craft such a book.

The Bible is so vast and complex, it tends to make humans uncomfortable. We want to simplify it, cut it down to size, to extract only what we think we need. We're lured to condense its message into talking points that are easier to manage. We take a slice out of the Bible-pie and then call it the pie.

When I've asked my more progressive Christian friends to tell me what the Bible is all about, they talk about the Exodus narrative, resistance to the empire, and God's heart for the poor. They've distilled that big book down to justice or liberation or subversion.

Some of my more conservative Christian friends focus on the ideas of God's holiness, our sinfulness, and the need for humans to be "set apart." They reduce the Bible's message to one of individual salvation and personal piety. As a result, they spend life trying to be as "good" as possible, using every opportunity to call others to righteousness, out of their "sinfulness" (as they define that by their reading of the Bible).

Who is right? To some extent, both are. They've each picked up on important biblical themes, but they've done so at the exclusion of others. The Bible has become more manageable in both cases, but it has been robbed of its magnitude and majesty, which rests on its being embraced as a whole.

I think about the infomercials for the late Jack LaLanne's Power Juicers that still run when only third-shift cashiers are watching. Imagine a pruny but strangely fit old man in a spandex bodysuit leaping around and declaring that the secret to long life is nothing more than fruit juice. Reaching into a silver bowl, he throws heaping handfuls of fruit and vegetables—carrots, apples, kale, bananas—into the hole atop his patented machine. The appliance gargles and grinds until it spits out a shot glass of muddy juice.

Christians have often done likewise when engaging the public square. Evangelicals, for example, often reduce the immense witness of the Scriptures to only a few culture-war issues—namely, abortion and gay marriage. Both are important issues deserving serious thought. The Scriptures speak often about life and sexuality. But they also regularly address poverty, equality, justice, peace, and care of God's good creation.

If Christians act as if the culture-war issues are the *only* issues or make them so paramount that they dwarf all others, we distill the limitless bounty of the Scriptures into a tiny cup of condensed political juice.

We are finite beings attempting to mine wisdom from the thoughts, commands, and actions of an infinite God. Believers know that the Bible equips us to offer a moral voice on many issues and should not try to force God's word to fit our purposes. When we err in this, the witness of God's Spirit resists our efforts by confronting us with its unbounded wisdom.

*   *   *

Some of today's leading Christian entities and voices show new life as they support "a broadening agenda." Still socially conservative on many issues, they feel called to attend to issues that most Christians haven't championed in the past.

For example, the great majority of young Christians still believe that abortion should be illegal in most or all cases.[1] At the same time, interest in social justice issues is growing among all Christians (especially young people).[2] According to in-depth research by LifeWay, 66 percent of young churchgoers claim that "social action is an extremely important part of their lives."[3] Yet, few believe they will see "a significant contribution" from current Christian leadership in addressing these issues.[4]

So some are taking matters into their own hands through broader advocacy efforts. A great example is my friend Tyler Wigg-Stevenson. Tyler believes that "God abhors the shedding of innocent blood,"[5] and he recognizes that nuclear weapons are unique vehicles for indiscriminate killing. If they are ever used in any circumstances, they will lead to massive loss of innocent life. Tyler believes Christians who value life and desire to follow a risen Jesus must oppose the existence of such weapons.

Reflecting on the Transfiguration, Tyler says, "Jesus had asked His disciples, 'What good will it be if a man gains the world but loses his own soul?' (Matthew 16:26). The power of our atomic age means that we have gained the world in a most literal sense. But at what cost—and what are we to do about it?"[6]

In 2009, he formed the Two Futures Project, a Christian organization fighting for the reduction, and ultimately, the abolition of nuclear weapons. And he is not a pie-in-the-sky dreamer on the margins. Tyler has gained support from Christian leaders, including the president of the National Association of Evangelicals, Leith Anderson, megachurch icons Bill and Lynne Hybels, and the editor in chief of *Christianity Today*, David Neff. What was viewed as a fringe "liberal" issue a generation ago is now finding traction among a diverse body of mainstream Christians.

This broadening agenda goes well beyond nuclear weapons. Bethany Hoang serves as director of the IJM Institute for International Justice Mission. IJM is a "human rights agency that secures justice for victims of slavery, sexual exploitation and other forms of violent oppression. IJM lawyers, investigators and aftercare professionals work with local governments to ensure victim rescue, to prosecute perpetrators and to strengthen the community and civic factors that promote functioning public justice systems."[7] Bethany believes her faith and the witness of Jesus Christ compel her to engage this work.

She writes,

> All throughout our lives Jesus offers sign-posts of the life-giving death that he wants to give to us. His grace and

promise of abundant life comes to us, more often than we would anticipate, through experiences that look like and echo the sounds of death...God gives us the gift of drawing us toward realities where death seems to reign, so that He can show us the power of the life He alone has to offer. This is witness. This is mission. Not merely to tell people that they can be raised from death to life, but to go to the places where death rules the day and let God use us to bring life, to show that Jesus has conquered all death.[8]

Organizations like Food for the Poor, World Vision, Compassion International, and adoption groups like Bethany Christian Services are flourishing. Established organizations like the National Association of Evangelicals and publications like *Christianity Today* now address issues ranging from the sanctity of life to global poverty to environmental stewardship—issues that should transcend party politics.

Traditionally conservative book publishers like InterVarsity Press, Zondervan, and Baker Books are providing a multiplicity of titles they arguably wouldn't have offered even a few decades ago.[9]

The church is waking up to the inadequacies of a public witness where a few issues get all the attention and the others fall by the wayside. Should the church fight for the lives of the unborn? Absolutely. But can Christians afford to ignore the 3 million already-living who will die from preventable water-related diseases this year? What about the 1.2 billion people without access to safe drinking water? And what of the tens of millions of orphans crying out from filthy beds in musty orphanages or the 1-million-plus Africans who will unnecessarily die of malaria in the next 12 months? How do we plan to address the plight of the poor in America's inner cities and the systemic injustices of our education system? Does an embrace of the full biblical witness lead us to a myopic agenda that pays these issues little more than lip service? Today's Christians know we can do better on a whole range of issues.

*   *   *

This broadening agenda has led to another mark of rising believers: political diversity. As Christian scholar David Gushee observed, a growing number of today's Christians share a "commitment to political independence and avoidance of partisan entanglements and their negative consequences."[10] They want to become co-laborers with God. They aren't trying to ride into the kingdom on the back of an elephant or a donkey.

Growing up, I thought being Democrat and Christian were mutually exclusive. I'm sure some on the other side felt the same way about being Republican. Today, I'm convinced that being Christian may mean eschewing party labels so that none but Christ can claim Christians as slaves.

In Jesus' day, every great religious teacher had a posse— what the Bible calls "disciples." This cohort of people follow a leader's teachings, adopt his views, and often do his bidding. One day, a group of Pharisees sent their disciples to Jesus to trap Him. "Teacher," they said, "we know that you are a man of integrity and that you teach the way of God in accordance with the truth. You aren't swayed by others, because you pay no attention to who they are. Tell us then, what is your opinion? Is it right to pay the imperial tax to Caesar or not?"[11]

To modern readers, this inquiry may seem harmless enough. In first-century Israel, however, it was loaded. The Jewish people were under oppression, and there was a growing movement of Jews who wanted nothing to do with the emperor. Yet Jesus sided neither with the oppressive Roman government nor with the Jewish politicians striving for independence. Maybe it was because Jesus knew that when people begin placing great faith in political groups, they may easily lose focus on Him, the ultimate answer to our world's problems.

This wasn't acceptable to the partisan Jews who wanted to throw the Romans out, to rebel, to take back their country for God. They didn't even want to pay imperial taxes. By asking this question, they were saying, "Whose side are you on—Rome's or Israel's?" The question is analogous to the way many Christians act during an election year, surveying the church parking lot to see which candidate's sticker is on which bumper.

Jesus sees their intentions for what they are and refuses to play their game. He tells them to bring Him a coin. Jesus asks, "Whose image is this? And whose inscription?"

"Caesar's," they replied.

Then He said to them, "Give back to Caesar what is Caesar's, and to God what is God's."[12]

When they heard this, the Scripture says, they left "amazed." Jesus wasn't going to let anyone put Him into a partisan box. His agenda was to do whatever the Father desired, and He wasn't going to co-opt God into a political agenda. Jesus eschews their labels and avoids their traps, and it shocks them. When Christians do the same in our day, they should expect similar responses.

Not long ago, a newspaper reporter asked me whom I voted for in the last presidential election. I declined to answer. She pressed me again. I told her I couldn't answer that question because I wasn't sure Jesus would respond if He were sitting in my seat. I was half-joking, but she asked for clarification.

Jesus came to earth in a time when Israel was dealing with its own partisan unrest. They were struggling with how to relate to a government that did not honor their community's values. After reading the Gospels and considering the way Jesus responded, I wasn't convinced the Son of God could claim either party were He alive today.

I think He would be a new kind of "values voter"—one who might offer support on moral issues no matter which party claimed ownership over it. The interviewer was floored, explaining that in all her years of religious reporting, she couldn't remember a single interviewee who refused to answer a question about party affiliation—certainly not based on a faith conviction.

Many Christians have now followed suit, refusing to align with either side. These changes make today's Christian movement so hard to grasp that when *Newsweek* wanted to name some of its top leaders, they produced an eclectic list of people who did not have much in common with each other. Among those named were vanguard conservatives like Princeton's Robert George and Tony Perkins of the Family Research

Council, leftist Jim Wallis, centrist Joel Hunter, and creation-care advocates Matthew and Nancy Sleeth. Not exactly the homogenous leadership of yesteryear.[13]

Rather than red or blue, many Christians tend to be a comfortable shade of purple. They are tired of an entrenched public witness that seeks to villainize, demonize, and destroy those perceived as the enemy, rather than listen to, learn from, and love our neighbors. They are weary of a culture-war mentality that speaks without listening, divides rather than unites, and promotes destructive partisanship.

Some of us have become nomads, political orphans who care more about living a life consistent with the teachings and ministry of Jesus Christ than toeing a particular party line. As activist Shane Claiborne says, a new generation of "political misfits" is rising from the ranks of the church community. These individuals are socially conservative but globally aware— more "conservative" on some issues and more "liberal" on others. Rather than a swelling religious Left, Claiborne says, we're witnessing the advent of the religious "stuck-in-the-middle."[14]

Rejecting the labels and even the culture wars themselves, many of today's Christians are carving out a new path that winds back and forth through the public square. And perhaps that is exactly where Christians need to be.

* * *

In the past couple of years, God has been convicting me of the church's poor witness on environmental issues. I've written numerous articles and even a book on what I've been learning from the Scriptures on this issue. On more than one occasion,

I've been asked, "Why do you write so much on creation care and not on an *important issue like abortion?*" (If they were familiar with the full body of my writing, they'd know that I *have* written on that issue, and more than once.) I always respond that I desire to hear a symphony of Christian voices speaking out about a host of moral issues.

I lean on the words of the Apostle Paul, who spoke of the church as the Body of Christ. A faith community, though made up of individual souls, exists as one body. Just like physical human bodies, this spiritual body has many parts. A foot is not any less a part of the body because it is not a hand. Hands need feet to travel where they want to go just as feet need hands to do something when they get there. If the whole body were made up of eyes, it might see, but it could not hear. Likewise, if the whole body were ears, it would hear through visual darkness. God has placed each part in the body exactly where it should be. Therefore, Paul concludes, no part can say to another, "I don't need you."[15]

Paul is speaking about spiritual gifts and how they should function within the larger church. Christians are best served, he contends, when all their individual gifts function together. A church of only teachers or only miracle workers is a lopsided church. He points out that our propensity is to assume that others should possess the same gifts we do, and he warns against those who look on the differently gifted with condescension.

As with spiritual gifts, so too with physical gifts and passions that are also distributed by the Spirit. Some today are exceptionally concerned for the poor, gifted by God to champion that work. Others are passionate about peacemaking, and they may choose to devote a portion of their lives or even their vocations to educating the church or fighting against unnecessary declarations of war. As the Puritans used to say, God breaks every heart differently.

The Scriptures call the peacemaker to care for the poor and the poverty advocate to be a peacemaker, but their lives may not be spent addressing each with equal vigor or time. The peacemaker must not look on the poverty advocate with disdain, and the poverty advocate should resist the urge to resent the peacemaker. Christians should not desire that every person work on one issue and not another. When the church sings in symphonic stereo, the sound is beautiful.

When I am tempted to turn up my nose at other Christians—yes, even culture-warring ones—who offer their witness in a way that differs from mine, I think about the navy blue codex from my childhood. Between its bonded leather covers sit 66 books with 1,189 chapters and 31,103 verses, each one expressing something of our Creator's character and speaking into our lives. I realize I can either throw this book into my spiritual juicer and attempt to force everyone to drink from my tiny glass, or let it be what it is, a vast and varied book with more wisdom than I might ever acquire on this side of eternity.

SIX

Faith at the Seams

I wasn't just asking questions; I was being changed by them.

—Wendell Berry, *Jayber Crow*

I've always struggled with faith. At each natural disaster or death or tragedy, I find myself wrestling with God. Every time God waits to answer my prayer, every time I encounter something that doesn't fit into the way I've systematized my own faith, I contend with that One whose answers always seem to be just outside my reach. I've learned to sit loosely in my faith and make room to revisit it again and again.

Most people experience moments like these. Times when something unexpected captures our spirit and stops life in its tracks. Times when we are brought low, when we wonder if much of what we thought we knew is actually true, when we feel like children again. In these moments, our minds take note of the images they process and our hands are aware of what they touch. I've experienced these times most often in my life when I've been overseas on mission trips.

A few years ago, I was in Brazil with some friends from my church. We were working in Juiz de Fora, a dusty, dirty mountain town where torn newspapers and empty candy wrappers danced in the streets. We were helping to plant churches and ministering among the impoverished. Many of the town's children lacked access to quality education and others were forced out of school to work at a young age to provide for their families. The cycle of poverty churned.

We were given a number of projects to choose from, and I chose to go to the orphanage. I didn't hear much about orphans growing up. My interaction with them boiled down to a videocassette of *The Newsies* that my brothers and I watched nonstop for a year or two. On occasion, a few orphans might show up on a Saturday infomercial during childhood, but this selfish child couldn't understand why they took up channel space that should be filled with cartoons.

My encounter in Brazil, however, was nothing like what I'd gathered it might be like from television. The faces of these children were soft and sweet. Somehow, amidst their mud homes and dirt floors, these children were able to wrangle up more joy than many American kids I know. We hugged and played with them and taught them Bible stories, and I realized why Jesus loved children so much. Why He identified with "the least of these." Staring into their eyes, I almost caught a glimpse of the Savior Himself.

The day we left the orphanage for the last time, our collective hearts were shot through with suffering. A girl gave another team member a note begging her to adopt her and become her "mommy." On the eternal ride back to the hotel, my friends and I sobbed as we passed around the note, trying to block out the image of the crying child being held back by an orphanage worker as we slid shut the van door.

All day and into dinner, I feigned joy even though my soul begged me to cry. Sliding into bed, I stared at blank pages in my journal, wondering how to give this story the words it deserved. I finally tossed the book back into my suitcase, determining it was best kept in my heart for now. I closed my eyes, but I could still see the image of the girl begging us to take her, to give her a home, to offer her a person to call "mommy" and "daddy."

I searched through the cabinet in my mind under "Christianity," but there wasn't a faith file in which to place this, no equipment to process it. Faith meant preaching tough sermons, evangelizing people, defending the truth against all the false teachers and opposing secularists who hated Jesus. My faith didn't say much about how to help this little girl.

Three years later, I had a similar experience, this time in Tanzania. I was helping facilitate a training seminar for pastors at an evangelical church outside the capital city of Dar es Salaam. I felt a little bit like a sixth grader trying to tell his father how to manage his 401(k). Many of the pastors attending this seminar had spent decades on the front lines of ministry. I had served in a church for just over one year. They were thriving spiritually in a region where Muslims outnumber Christians almost two to one. I had spent life on Christian cruise control in the American Bible Belt. They should have been teaching me.

I slipped behind the church to stand on the banks of a narrow river and wallow in my inadequacies. The fumes from the polluted river assaulted my nostrils. Old automobile tires, potato chip bags, and aerosol cans were piled high in its waters.

To my right, I saw a child in a tattered shirt naked from the waist down. Calloused bare feet carried him across the rocky dirt road to the river's bank. Steadying himself with the help of a tree, he began urinating. My eyes followed the flow through the rubbish rapids to a young woman—probably no more than 30 years old—removing a large jar from atop her head to collect water. Perhaps she would use it to make stew for the family or maybe she'd offer it to her children. I didn't know.

My first impulse was to rush over and stop her. She needed to know the chemicals leaking from the breakdown of the tires were toxic, that a child had just urinated upstream. But she already knew. She saw what I saw, but she had no choice.

Standing between a half-naked child urinating in this river and a young woman collecting her household's share of daily water, I thought, *If the Christian faith doesn't have an answer for this, what good is it?*

* * *

As I've dialogued with other Christians, I've discovered that many today have had similar experiences. Whether on the mission field in a South American slum or working in an inner-city soup kitchen or watching an in-depth report about the Sudanese genocide, they were confronted with a problem that neither their theology nor their politics could answer. These moments make them question what they believe. They realize that some political and theological perspectives thrive in middle-class suburban enclaves, but crumble in other contexts. Standing face-to-face with suffering or inequity or social ills, they realize that they can't continue to think, speak, or behave as they once did.

These experiences—these faith crises—are often the turbines behind the shifts taking place in our culture. Experiences like these thrust people of faith back into the Scriptures to ask new and different questions.

My friend Gary lives just across the Georgia border in Alabama. He describes himself as a "conservative with open eyes." By this, he means that he leans to the right politically on most things, but he often deviates from this paradigm when confronted with a great need that his systematized conservatism can't answer. What caused him to begin thinking this way? An experience among the poor in South America.

"I was the staunchest Rush Limbaugh–style conservative until I went to Venezuela and stood on a two-mile-long garbage dump where children were foraging for food," Gary told me. "I realized that all the things I believed in—limited government, everyone taking care of themselves, pulling yourself up by your bootstraps—were useless at that moment. None of it was going to fix the problem."

Then there's my friend Tony, a former Presbyterian minister from Tennessee. He and his wife were typical evangelicals who loved Jesus, football, and Ronald Reagan—the evangelical holy trinity. A few years ago, they decided to adopt a physically handicapped child from overseas.

The day Tony and his wife landed in Guatemala, they headed to a luxurious five-star hotel where they met their child, Esther, for the first time. Her brown skin and innocent two-year-old face charmed them. As the orphanage representative supervised, they hugged and played with her. They loved her as if she were already their own. Finally, they headed to the orphanage to finalize the paperwork. In an instant, Tony recalls going from the most luxurious place he'd ever been in his life to the most destitute.

When they entered the courtyard, they saw 20 special-needs children slumped over in high chairs where they sat all day. Their faces were devoid of life; they didn't even turn to look at visitors. Stepping through an open door, Tony and his wife entered the baby room. Suddenly, Esther started screaming and burying her head in Tony's leg. He looked around to see children crammed together in cribs, wrapped in unchanged diapers. Few cried, knowing they would not be helped, and many were malnourished. Tony learned later that one of these children starved to death two weeks after their visit.

"That was the single moment in my life where everything came crashing down. It was like a television show where the white light flashes and the actor sees their life sweep before their eyes in a microsecond," Tony said. "As a minister, I saw a flash of church budgets and building projects and all the wasted money. I thought to myself, 'Am I a liberal now?'"

As a conservative evangelical, Tony believed he was supposed to care about evangelism and leave social issues to liberals.

"My politics said everyone was supposed to take care of themselves. I remember saying, 'The liberals give out a cup of cold water; we give out the living water,'" he said. "But if everyone simply takes care of themselves, who will take care of these kids? All of a sudden, I wanted to be the one giving out the cup of cold water. Something needed to change."

Something *did* change. After Tony and his wife returned home, he quit his comfy church job and went to work for a Christian adoption agency. Today, he educates churches on the biblical basis for orphan care and has recalibrated his political views.

According to inertia, a resting object will remain at rest unless acted upon by an outside force. As it turns out, these faith crisis moments are the outside forces pushing many Christians today to reconsider the way they are living out their faith in the public square. Sometimes these are experienced in international contexts, but often they occur in the rhythm of our daily routines. Sometimes it comes in an epiphany while reading the Scriptures or a flash of clarity in a conversation with a friend that challenges you to be more thoughtful about what you believe and why.

* * *

Nowhere has the impact of these faith crisis moments been more apparent than on same-sex relationship issues. They are among the most divisive and explosive culture-war hot buttons. Far more complicated than we sometimes admit, these matters are charged with emotion and often deeply personal. In the past, some Christians could feel far removed from gay and lesbian people. But as a new generation navigates a world in which homosexuality is more publicly accepted, this is changing.

My straight friend Brad from Orlando unwittingly moved into a gay neighborhood while he was in college a few years ago. He calls it the "gayborhood," and what he found there surprised him. His neighbors were kind and generous, not at all similar to the caricatures of crusading, entitled activists he often heard about. "They were so different than I thought. They were real."

God led him to the neighborhood for another reason. A couple of years after he moved there, his father divorced his mom and told the family he was gay. "I realized God was not only chastening me on the way I thought about and treated gays. He was preparing me for that moment."

Like Brad, I had my own revelatory moment on this issue. My friend Shawn and I grew up in church together. We both sang in youth choir, and neither of us missed a church service. He was somewhat reserved but seemed happy. When I moved away to college, we lost touch. I went to Virginia and he to North Carolina.

After college, we both returned to the same town and the same church. I was interning with our young-adult ministry, but he was distant from our community. Withdrawn in conversation. Stoic. When Shawn showed up for Bible study, I'd notice him staring off in the distance as his mind wandered.

One Sunday after church, he asked me if we could meet for dinner. Before we could review the menu, Shawn looked at me and announced, "I'm gay."

"How did this happen?" I asked, thinking, as so many do, that some precipitating event renders one gay or lesbian.

"It didn't *happen*," he said. "It's always been this way."

I didn't know what to say. A rush of clichés I'd picked up in church flowed into my mind, but I was pretty sure telling him "God didn't create Adam and Steve" wasn't going to help anything. I sat in silence.

Shawn told me that when he was about 13, he noticed his attraction to males. He'd tried praying and reading his Bible when he felt these urges, but that didn't help much. Blistering sermons on homosexuality only made him feel worse.

He sank into depression before confessing his secret to his parents. They sent him to therapy, hoping to make him straight. The sessions reinforced his belief that he was sick, perverted, and gross.

In college, he sought help through various campus ministries, but they were unequipped for the task. The ministers told him that sexuality was a choice; he just needed to choose a different path. They prescribed more Bible reading and prayer. Shawn slipped into deeper desperation, even tried having sex with girls as an effort to "be normal." Looking down at the table and shuffling silverware, he said that the church had no place for him and that his Christian friends would never understand, so he was going to try living according to who he felt he was.

Over dinner, he poured out his frustrations and struggles and pain—often in more detail than I was prepared to handle. We didn't talk much about theology, and we didn't attempt to exegete Leviticus 18. Those paths were well worn in his life. Instead, I let years of emotions spill out of his heart onto the table and reminded him, "Shawn, I'm still your friend."

Shawn left our church. I'd call and leave messages or email him, but he rarely answered. I heard from a friend that he had moved downtown, but I didn't know where. All I could do was wait.

More than one year later, my phone rang.

"Jonathan, it's Shawn."

"Hey man," I said. "It's good to hear your voice. I've been trying to get in touch with you."

He said he'd had a lot going on so he hadn't found time to call me, but he was reaching out now because his birthday was coming up. He wanted to know if I would come to his party, but before I committed he needed to let me know that there would be a lot of gay people there. He said he understood if I didn't feel comfortable attending.

Trying to hide my discomfort, I said, "I'll be there."

Hanging up the phone, I wondered what I'd gotten myself into. *How was I going to go to a birthday party in a house full of gay people? What if my friends found out? What if someone posted a picture on Facebook and I was visible in the background? How would I explain this to all my church friends?*

I realized why so many Christians spend so little time with gays and lesbians. As Christians have marginalized gay and lesbian relationships and lifestyles, they've marginalized the community itself, making them modern-day lepers, the new unclean. Christians stay as far away from them as possible. I didn't want to live that way. I loved my friend too much, and I made up my mind I wouldn't let Christian social stigmas drive me out of his life.

When I arrived at Shawn's party, the house was full of men, none of whom I'd met before. I assumed most were gay so I kept my eye contact to a minimum and my conversations short. Making my way to the kitchen, I saw Shawn, who greeted me with a surprised look.

"I didn't think you'd actually show up," he said, "but I'm glad you're here."

Shawn turned down the music and yelled, "Hey everyone, this is Jonathan. He's my Christian friend. Try to make him feel welcome."

They did. I relaxed, and conversation flowed freely. Contrary to my preconceptions, they didn't stand around chatting about gay bars and leather and *Will and Grace*. They were real people with jobs and hobbies. We talked about music and movies and, yes, even sports. My evening was going surprisingly well until a guy named Dave asked me what he believed was a harmless question: "So, Jonathan, where'd you go to college?"

I wanted to climb under my seat, but I was standing up.

"I went...um...I went to Liberty University."

A shout came from across the room: "Wait. Isn't that Jerry Falwell's school?"

"Yes."

Conversations ceased. Bodies went motionless. No one knew what to say. In some Christian circles, a degree from Liberty generates respect. It serves as my membership card, proving I am a part of the conservative Christian club. But in this room it dredged up pain and fury. Dissatisfaction seeped from the eyes of the other guests, most of whom were now quietly focused on our conversation.

"When I was a child, I stumbled on a news story about Jerry Falwell," Dave said. He looked at the floor now, and I could tell he was pre-selecting his words.

> The article was about a lawsuit that had been filed against Falwell by a gay man. He'd referred to homosexuals as "brute beasts" and said churches that accepted gay people were a "vile and Satanic system that will one day be utterly annihilated, and there will be a celebration in heaven." I was already aware of my sexual orientation when I read the story. I decided then and there that I would never, ever walk inside the door of a Christian church. Not for a wedding, not for a funeral, not for anything. And I never have.[1]

He looked back into my face, squaring off to say something I knew would be tough to hear.

> Tell me, Jonathan. How can I go to a place where people think I am a monster? And how can I even consider worshipping a God who would celebrate my annihilation?

Tears pooled in the corner of his eyes. And mine. His honesty unraveled me.

Pushing through the embarrassment, I made an attempt to apologize, saying that not all Christians thought that way. But my words didn't seem to console. Hate speech had singed his soul. Far more than an apology was needed to heal the wound.

For me, for Brad, and for an entire generation of Christians, experiences with hurting people like these have made it clear how deeply the church has failed the gay and lesbian community. Same-sex issues seem simple outside of any meaningful connection to the people involved. They take on a whole new shape when considered in the context of our friends and family.

Driving home that night, I decided I didn't care who knew where I'd been or if my picture showed up on Facebook. I was not going to contribute to the dehumanization of this community any longer, and I was going to do what I could to raise awareness about the tragic witness of the Christian church on homosexuality.

. . . .

Christians—myself included—have allowed our leaders to spew hatred at a community of people who are no more sinful and no less precious than the most pious. In the past, we remained silent as many prominent Christian leaders declared that AIDS was God's final judgment on homosexuals. We turned a blind eye to so-called Christian counselors who performed extreme and abusive fix-a-gay therapies that included techniques like electrical shock and masturbatory reconditioning in attempts to make gay people straight. Christians have often spoken of gays and lesbians as if they have some sort of medical disease that has been diagnosed and can be cured with a simple biblical prescription.

Too many Christians allow their teenagers to use the terms "gay" or "faggot" interchangeably with "stupid" or "loser." They keep quiet when pastors preach harshly about sexual struggles while they play sermonic patty-cake with issues like gossip, divorce, greed, and lust that run rampant in their own congregations. Is it any wonder that many churches have no out-of-the-closet gays attending but enough out-of-the-closet gluttons to fill up a dozen church buses?

Even the most conservative culture warriors recognize our failures. "We've practiced what can only be described as a form of homophobia," says Albert Mohler, president of the Southern Baptist Theological Seminary. "We've used the 'choice' language when it is clear that sexual orientation is a deep inner struggle and not merely a matter of choice."[2]

The mantra of many Christians over the last quarter century has been "hate the sin, love the sinner." But if you search the web for public statements made by Christians regarding their homosexual neighbors, you'll uncover a long history of hating sin and little if anything about loving sinners.[3] To wit:

- Televangelist Jimmy Swaggart once said, "If a gay man ever hit on me, I'd kill him and tell God he died."
- Presbyterian pastor D. James Kennedy reacted to a notion of gays serving in the military by sending out a letter asking, "Honestly, would you want your son, daughter, or grandchild sharing a shower, foxhole, or blood with a homosexual?"
- Founder of the Christian Broadcasting Network Pat Robertson declared that for him, "[homosexuality] is sodomy. It is repugnant."

- Ten Commandments crusader and Alabama judge Roy Moore called homosexuality an "abhorrent, immoral, detestable crime against nature" that should be punishable by law.[4]
- E. Calvin Beisner of the Christian Cornwall Alliance wrote an article arguing against the "militant homosexuals" who were calling for an increase in federal spending on AIDS research, treatment, and education. Beisner asked if it was "rational" to increase funding to "fight a disease that is almost 100 percent self-inflicted by people intent on immoral and irrational behavior? Not when there are more pressing matters that ought to take priority."[5]
- Tony Perkins of Family Research Council actually opposed anti–gay bullying legislation, arguing that "the homosexual movement" was causing gay youth suicides, and was now "exploiting these tragedies."[6]
- David Barton, a go-to historian for many conservatives, argues that the United States should ban gays from the military because the founders would have. As examples of apparently laudable policy, Barton argued that George Washington "was the first not only to forbid, but even to punish homosexuals in the military," and that Thomas Jefferson "authored a bill penalizing sodomy by castration."[7] He has also asked, "Why don't we regulate homosexuality?" comparing gay men and lesbians to trans fats, fast food, cigarettes, hard liquor, and salt.[8]

I've heard more sermons on the sinfulness of homosexuality than I can recall, but I can't remember one quibble from a Christian friend or pastor over any of these statements. Yet, every Christian I know agrees that we must love gays and lesbians. As the Apostle John reminds us, loving someone in mere words rather than actions isn't love at all.[9]

If we say we love our gay and lesbian neighbors, but then allow our leaders to speak hatred toward them, our hypocrisy is exposed and people suffer. Gay teens, for example, are now six times more likely to attempt suicide than their heterosexual peers,[10] and many believe religious messages are partly at fault.[11] More than four in five Americans give churches low marks when it comes to handling this issue.[12]

Americans recognize that the church's unloving, unproductive political activity has often been based on sentiments diametrically opposed to those of one prominent religious leader: Jesus. A vast chasm separates the life of Jesus and the lives of many who claim to follow Him when it comes to loving the marginalized and broken.

Even non-Christians know Jesus was compassionate toward every kind of sinner. Prostitutes, drunks, and, worst of all, tax collectors—they were some of Jesus' closest friends. While the religious aristocracy of Jesus' day was finding new ways to express sin-hate, Jesus was busy loving every sinner He could find.

The contrast between twenty-first-century Christianity and the Jesus of the Bible is stark. This Jesus—the compassionate, loving friend of sinners—is difficult to reconcile with an often disconnected, insular "us-versus-them" Christianity. Jesus said His disciples would be known by their love, but in America today they are known in part for their anger toward homosexuals. A shocking 91 percent of young people in America now say they perceive Christians as "anti-gay."[13]

. . .

Today's Christians are uniquely positioned to infuse the conversation about same-gender relationships that is taking place in the political arena with love and grace because they are in a closer relationship with gays and lesbians. For example, 37 percent of evangelicals ages 18 to 34 say they have a close friend or relative who is homosexual. Only 16 percent of evangelicals 35 and older can say the same.[14] Fighting a faceless agenda is easier than warring against a friend.

Many Christians have witnessed firsthand how this community has suffered as societal pariahs at the hands of misinformed Christians who believe gays and lesbians chose their sexual orientation. Though many Christians still believe that God desires a better path for the lives of gays and lesbians, these Christians also understand that our obligation to love them is not dependant on their capitulation to a particular belief system. It is impossible for these Christians to lump every homosexual into "the gay agenda" and claim they all want to destroy the fabric of our society. (It's a classic culture-war tactic: publicize the most extreme flank and then use that caricature to falsely represent the larger community. They pretend that the most fanatical voices in a community represent them all.)

When I hear young Christians discuss homosexuality, they speak with more compassion, sympathy, and love than has been common in the past. Christians must balance their convictions with the scriptural understanding that *all* have sinned.

Individuals who follow Christ have not ceased to be sinners; they are sinners who have taken advantage of God's gracious gift of salvation. As one writer correctly observes:

> The Christian argument against homosexuality has changed. It used to be, "Gays are really only messed-up straight people. They should let Jesus make them straight, so that they can stop acting all gay and not go to hell." *Now* the argument is "A homosexual struggling against the temptation to act homosexual is no different from anyone else struggling to resist a sinful temptation."[15]

The most robust description of love in all of Scripture comes from 1 Corinthians 13, which says, "Love is patient and kind. Love is not jealous or boastful or proud or rude. It does not demand its own way. It is not irritable, and it keeps no record of being wronged."[16] If Christians' language were marked by these characteristics—humility, kindness, and grace—it would ease tensions and open up avenues for dialogue.

And it doesn't end with dialogue. Let us not forget that love is not only a noun, but a verb. Love is an action. Our assertions that we love our neighbors must be accompanied by tangible expressions of that love. Christians need to begin looking for ways to affirm, rather than undermine, their claims to love their homosexual neighbors.[17] And this is where the issue moves into the public square.

Young Christians are far more likely to support common-sense legislation on same-sex issues.[18] They support protections against violent hate crimes or discrimination in the workplace. Many even support cleaning up the legal cobwebs that govern hospital visitation rights and inheritances for gay couples.

Some culture-war groups oppose even minor concessions, claiming we should not "normalize" homosexuality in our culture.[19] They fail to realize that our role as Christians is not to delegitimize the existence of those who do not share our beliefs. Our job is to mirror Christ by loving people in spite of our differences and advocating for our culture's disenfranchised groups.

Christians are also increasingly supportive of same-sex unions. Even among conservative Protestants, 52 percent of young people already say they support some form of same-sex union.[20] According to Robert Jones, the president of Public Religion Research, the trends among Christians on same-sex issues such as unions all point in one direction, and the group should expect "sea change within a generation."

If he's right, this debate as we know it is over. Its demise can be attributed—at least partially—to Christians' transformative experiences among their gay friends. Being in relationship with homosexuals is one of the highest predictors of one's views on same-sex issues.[21] For better or for worse, the experiences of young Christians are causing a generation to rethink the way they've handled this issue.

This doesn't mean, however, that all young Christians are erasing the biblical lines on sexuality. While most Christians continue to hold that homosexual behaviors are morally wrong and God has a better path for our lives,[22] they are exploring new ways to show love for gay and lesbian neighbors—even in the public square. Christians don't need to compromise their convictions in order to love their neighbors.

The Christian position on sexuality and homosexual engagement that seems to be on the rise might be summed up best by Orthodox writer Frederica Mathewes-Green:

> I can believe that my gay friends are engaging in something spiritually damaging, without asking the law to stop them. They can perceive that my convictions are grounded in an ancient spiritual consensus, not hate. We still won't agree. But perhaps we can understand each other, and continue the conversation with mutual respect.[23]

This way of addressing the issue seems to draw us away from destructive, counterproductive culture-war tactics while leaving the Bible intact. It allows us to move beyond condemnation of the marginalized to the good news of Jesus Christ that sets us all free from our destructive ways.

Whether we're considering same-sex issues or global poverty, we can't deny the role that experience is playing in the formation of young Christians. My own experiences in this crazy, messed-up world tell me that we need to do a better job addressing the many problems we're facing. As I've sat across tables in coffee shops and attended birthday parties, my spiritual stitching has been pulled and stretched. After these moments, I often find myself poring over the Bible, sewing up my faith's split seams.

I believe Christians in our current era need more than a series of talking points or an organized agenda. Faith must be worked out through living—although experiences alone cannot be trusted. They must be interpreted through the lens of Christ and the Bible, which speaks of Him. Life should be lived, in the words of Karl Barth, with the Bible in one hand and the newspaper in the other.

SEVEN

Give Me the Songs of a Nation

A battle lost or won is easily described, understood, and appreciated, but the moral growth of a great nation requires reflection, as well as observation.

—FREDERICK DOUGLASS

I began November 20, 2009, like many others, browsing my favorite news sites when I stumbled on a *New York Times* headline that read "Christian Leaders Unite on Political Issues."

The article reported that more than 100 conservative evangelicals with a handful of Catholics and a few Eastern Orthodox priests had drafted a public manifesto with the intent of laying out a political framework for Christians. The "Manhattan Declaration" reaffirmed the signatories' belief in the importance of three hot-button issues: abortion, gay marriage, and religious liberty.

The signers were almost all older white males,[1] but their collective pedigree was impressive. Evangelical signers included James Dobson, Richard Land, Gary Bauer, and Tony Perkins.

They were joined by Princeton's Robert George, nine Roman Catholic archbishops, and the primate of the Orthodox Church in America.

As I read the *Times* article and the declaration itself, it became clear that the statement offered little new information. Conservative Christians saying they oppose abortion and gay marriage isn't exactly news, but it was interesting that they were attempting to speak to young people.[2]

"We argue that there is a hierarchy of issues," said Charles Colson, one of the principal drafters. "A lot of the younger evangelicals say they're all alike. We're hoping to educate them that these are the *three most important issues*."[3]

Colson's statement irritated me, but I decided to set that aside for a moment and consider his arguments. He and other conservatives noticed that many of today's Christians were engaging a broad range of issues like poverty, peacemaking, and environmentalism. Although he correctly diagnosed the problem, Colson failed to consider the *why* behind the *what*. And in so doing, he'd set out to instruct a generation in a way that would most assuredly not be heard.

The changing face of Christian political engagement is a story that has been told over and over again by the American media. While many observe what is going on, few seem to understand why this change is occurring. They observe the broadening agenda, growing political diversity, propensity for civil dialogue, and desire to work on common ground agendas among rising Christian leaders. But they haven't identified just why this shift is occurring at this moment and among this generation. I felt I needed to respond to Colson's mandate, but I also struggled to find the right words with which to do so.

* * *

As I've observed young Christians and considered my own changing perspective in recent years, there seem to be several reasons the movement is heading in a new direction. No one will deny that there is a *reaction* against the past several decades of Christian political engagement. They're embarrassed by the way our faith has been represented to a watching world as little more than a political movement.

"It's like our crazy Uncle Harry got out of the home and ran into city hall wearing a shirt with the family name," comments evangelical pastor Joel Hunter. "We love him, but he misrepresents us."[4]

A new generation of Christians has come of age in a globalized, über-connected society where retreating into an insulated, Christian subculture is no longer an option. They work, play, shop, and sip coffee with their friends and neighbors. They've seen how Christian leaders—especially those in the "Christian Right"—poorly represent the faith. They've witnessed the rancorous taste left in the mouths of those they care about. As a result, they've made up their minds to run in the opposite direction, to abandon the uncivil rhetoric, blind partisanship, pursuit of power, and culture-war tactics.

Not only is the Christian political witness of the past embarrassing, it has also been shown to be a failure. Two decades after conservative Christians rushed into partisan politics, one of the former leaders of the Religious Right acknowledged their failure. Millions of dollars were wasted, and the culture hadn't been morally restored. Reflecting on his political work, he says,

> It must now be acknowledged that we have failed. We failed not because we were wrong about our critique of culture, or because we lacked conviction, or because there were not enough of us, or because too many were lethargic and uncommitted. We failed because we were unable to redirect a nation from the top down. Real change must come from the bottom up or, better yet, from the inside out.[5]

Countless dollars and hours were poured into a Christian strategy to capture power and transform a nation through partisan politics. What is there to show for it? Almost no progress has been made on any of the culture-war hot buttons, and the infamous moral decline continues. Today's Christians have decided not to allow this legacy to extend any further because they see that this strategy has been neither helpful nor efficacious.

Considering this, young Christians may seem rash. But each generation is reacting in some way to those who came before them. This is a sociological phenomenon that plagues every generation in every age. Christians in the 1970s and 1980s who formed the Religious Right were reacting as well—to a culture that seemed to be abandoning traditional values and to Christians who misguidedly fled the public square. So if today's Christians are reacting—and to some degree they are—they are reacting to a reactive expression of faith.

In addition to reacting to the missteps of the previous iteration of Christian political engagement, today's Christians are *responding* to their own experiences and the world around them. Through the Internet, Christians are now able to witness and understand our world's problems in real time. If a new report is released on poverty in South Asia, or if an organization estimates the number of orphans globally, or if a tsunami strikes, the news races around the world to laptops in coffee shops from Tokyo to Toronto.

The ease of modern travel has also allowed rising Christians to witness these tragedies firsthand. Young Christians are more likely to take mission trips than older ones, and as a result,[6] they know what kinds of problems afflict those who reside outside our "God-blessed" borders.[7] As the Apostle James writes, "If anyone, then, knows the good they ought to do and doesn't do it, it is sin for them."[8] Previous generations may be somewhat excused for a narrower agenda, but this generation will not be. We've been assaulted by the world's ills—stories of poverty, hunger, genocide, disease, and unnecessary suffering occurring around the globe—and we can't ignore them.

Today's Christians aren't just addressing international problems. They are responding to experiences within their own communities. As they interact with others—from gay and lesbian friends to oppressed minorities struggling to survive in the inner city—they've found themselves standing in the tension of serious problems and a faith that's often ignored them.

Not long ago, I spent time with a Christian friend who works for a conservative Christian advocacy group. Somehow the conversation turned to the next generation, and he asked me a most insightful question.

"We know that young people tend to be more progressive and open-minded, but they often get more conservative as they age," he said. "Don't you think this young generation will wise up as they get older?"

He cited a quote often attributed to Winston Churchill: "If you're not a liberal at twenty five you have no heart; if you're not a conservative at thirty five you have no brain."[9]

Young people *do* tend to become more like their parents (read, "get more conservative") as they age. But the shift under consideration is not a liberal/conservative one. Rising Christians in America are quite conservative in many respects. And their embrace of issues that are considered "liberal" in America (e.g., environmentalism, justice, care for the poor, etc.) isn't the result of a youth rebellion.

As I've poked and prodded my friends and searched my own heart, I'm finding that the primary element driving the changes we're seeing is not reaction or response, but *reflection*. This is good because neither our experiences nor our emotions can be fully trusted. They can both be powerfully useful, not by forcing us to make snap judgments and risk overcorrecting, but by causing us to consider pressing questions with fresh eyes and reengage the word of God in our search for answers.

• • •

Driven by their desire to touch the world outside of the church's four walls, Christians have *reflected on culture* and the best ways to relate to it. A movement previously known for condemning and separating from anything considered "worldly" is now reconsidering how to engage, shape, and impact the world around it.

Inspired by the ministry of Jesus, Christians are now showing up in most "worldly" places, where they're forming deep friendships with non-believers and working to restore brokenness.[10] Rather than lamenting everything that is wrong with the world or retreating into a corner filled with Christian schools, Christian movies, Christian music, and alternative Halloween holidays, today's Christians are rushing into places where you wouldn't have found them a generation ago. They know you can't impact the world while holding it at arm's length.

Rather than get offended at our world's brokenness, Christians see these as opportunities. When they perceive a problem, they are less likely to mobilize an angry protest and more likely to begin working with others to create and implement solutions. Rather than focusing on what's wrong in culture and warring against it, they are cultivating goodness.

Such a shift in cultural engagement creates ripples in the way Christians think about and engage politics. Fueled in part as a reaction to our community's recent failures and in part by fresh reflections on culture, God's kingdom, and the gospel, today's Christians are reevaluating the intersection of faith and the public square. The paradigms that seemed to work yesterday have proved ineffective, and Christians are now forced to ask what it looks like to follow Jesus in a pluralistic, post-Christian reality.

Today's Christians are influenced by the thinking of scholars like James Davison Hunter and Michael Horton and practitioners like Mark Rodgers of The Clapham Group who've argued that culture is upstream of politics, that a country's laws are a function of the hearts and minds of its citizens. If you want to shape the government, they assert, shape the people who empower that government. As Damon of Athens said, "Give me the songs of a nation and it does not matter who writes its laws."

A vivid picture of this paradigm shift comes from the acclaimed Christian author Philip Yancey. He visited Moscow in 1991, just as the Soviet Union was crumbling under the weight of its own insufficiencies, to meet with the editors of the Communist magazine *Pravda*. The publication had fallen from a circulation of 11 million to around 700,000, and the editors were now seeking advice from a faith their movement's founder had called "the opiate of the people."

The editors remarked to Yancey that they believed Communism and Christianity shared many of the same ideals—among them were justice, compassion, and equality—yet Communism had become a nightmare while Christianity continued to flourish.

"We don't know how to motivate people to show compassion," the editor in chief commented. "We tried raising money for the children of Chernobyl, but the average Russian would rather spend his money on drink. How do you reform and motivate people? How do you get them to be good?"

For nearly a century, Soviet Communism tried to legislate its brand of morality with laws, regulations, and even the prodding of bayonets. All it produced was poverty, rebellion, and a society that was less virtuous and less moral than when the political paradigm was first instituted. Confronting the flaws of the Kremlin forced Yancey to confront his own assumptions as an American Christian.

"I came away from Russia with the strong sense that we Christians would do well to relearn the basic lesson of [Christ's wilderness] Temptation," he reflected. "Goodness cannot be imposed externally, from the top down; it must grow internally, from the bottom up."[11]

This is not to say that Christians should not be involved in the public square, that they should not be a faithful presence there as in other spheres of culture. Government can be a powerful tool for justice and goodness, and often Christians must advocate for policies that punish injustice, restrain evil, and promote a healthier society. But for the Christian, politics is not the only tool or even the primary tool of change.

"In a free society, government reflects the soul of its people. If people want change at the top, they will have to live in different ways. Our major social problems are not the cause of our decadence. They are a reflection of it," says commentator Cal Thomas. He goes on to note, "While we work toward legislation, we must also do the more difficult task of changing people's minds and beliefs on the matter. The most effective laws *follow* moral consensus—they do not bring about moral consensus."[12]

Sentiments like Thomas's are penetrating the broader Christian consciousness and changing the way many think about the public square. Politics can never change hearts, and the next generation seems more interested in winning hearts than in winning the culture wars. Rather than simply lobby for just laws, they also want to act justly and to cultivate a desire for justice among our citizenry. Instead of claiming to believe in the sanctity of life, they want to partner with others to save lives, protect lives, and cultivate a shared value for life throughout the world. As rising Christians reflect on culture, they are engaging the world in new and fresh ways.[13]

Additionally, today's Christians have *reflected on the Bible*. This might sound odd at first, as if I'm saying that previous generations pushed the Bible aside and pursued their own ends while rising Christians take God's word seriously. This is not what I mean. Rather, today's Christians approach the Bible with fresh eyes, as each generation must.

When Christians from modernist generations approached the Bible, they often led with rationalism. I experienced this approach to the Bible growing up in the evangelical world, where God's word was seen as a set of propositional truth statements, logically laid out and easy to interpret if you knew what you were doing. If you wanted to know what to believe or do or how to respond to something, you just found the verse in the Bible that told you and put it in your pocket.[14]

But rising generations—perhaps as a result of the influence of postmodernism—are falling in love with the Bible's overarching *narrative*. That's why so many people today talk about "the story of God" or the Bible's "grand narrative." Not that they are rejecting the idea that the Bible holds propositional truths or are fleeing biblical literalism—they aren't[15]—rather, they want to enter the Bible, wrestle with its full message, and try to embody it daily.

Why is this significant? Because every story has a climax, and today's Christians are convinced that the climax of the Bible's narrative is Jesus.[16] Everything in the Scriptures points to Christ and everything speaks of Christ. He stands with God at the Creation, is surprisingly sewn throughout the Old Testament, is the subject of the Gospels, and Paul begins almost every letter by invoking His name. For a growing number of rising Christians, He is also the paradigm through which they are reading the Bible anew. If Christians are shifting, a re-acquainting with the person and work of Jesus is almost certainly behind it.[17]

This is more than a theological nuance, for when theology is lived (as it always should be), it seeps out of every pore and spills onto our lives. If we take seriously the "follow me" call of Christ, where will it lead us? To the picket line wearing a sandwich board? Or into the soup kitchen, where we touch and heal and feed? If we read the Bible through the lens of the biblical Jesus, it changes the way we live, even down to our advocacy in the public square.

Take the issue of war, for example. As I've dialogued with older Christians about war, they almost always offer the same answer. They head over to Romans 13 and retrieve the Scripture about government being given the power of the sword. But as I talk to younger Christians, they want to know how to read Romans 13 through the prism of a Jesus who blesses peacemakers and loves enemies. Most do not reject the idea that the government has the right to wield the sword, but they believe Christians should resist it if at all possible and stand behind it weeping when it must be wielded. As Christians enter into the Bible in new ways and read its truth with fresh eyes, this generation is coming away with different approaches to life, ministry, and even politics.

Perhaps related to the other two, today's Christians are *reflecting on the gospel* and what it means to proclaim and live that out in our world. A fresh vision for understanding, articulating, even "rediscovering" the gospel is emerging in the Christian community. Just check out the Christian section at your local bookstore (if one still stands in your town). A quick perusal in my own revealed the following titles:

- *The Naked Gospel*
- *What Is the Gospel?*
- *The Rest of the Gospel*
- *Counterfeit Gospels*
- *The Gospel for Real Life*
- *The Gospel According to Jesus*
- *The Hole in Our Gospel*

Christians today seem determined to understand what the gospel is and what it's not. What Jesus' gospel meant, and how we manipulate it to fit our purposes. Which "gospels" are false, and how the real one should interact with our lives.

But while there may be some minor disagreement among the authors of each of these books, I'm finding a common thread throughout that is tying together a new generation of Christians. Almost everyone seems to agree that the Christian gospel is, in the words of the Apostle Paul, "of first importance."[18]

They all recognize that this gospel, this story of Jesus that is good news for the world, should be paramount.

When forecasting the future of American Christianity, Gabe Lyons notes that for a new generation the gospel "is the foundational assertion of the Bible—the driving motivation for everything they do."[19] In his book *The Next Christians*, the word "gospel" appears more than 100 times.

More than being central to their theology, the gospel has become integrated into their entire lives. It informs their sense of vocation, the way they're spending their free time, the causes they support, and even the way they consume goods. They believe the gospel of Jesus should inform all of life (to borrow a phrase from Francis Schaeffer). A new generation is not content to silo the gospel, to constrict it to what happens on the mission field or in a church during Sunday services. They integrate it into the fabric of their lives. That includes the way today's Christians think about and engage politics.

Take the issue of adoption, for example. This has become the cause du jour among many in the church today. The easy approach to this is to point to the apostle James, who tells us to "care for widows and orphans," and then go do that. But that's not the approach taken by many today. They are asking an even bigger, perhaps more difficult, question: How does the gospel of Jesus Christ inform our care of orphans?

As adoption advocate Russell Moore points out, it is because of the gospel that we who were spiritual orphans are made sons and daughters of God. And then he asks, "If that is true, for those of us who believe the gospel, then why would we not be those who above all people around us are willing to be those who show what it means for orphans to be made beloved children?"[20] The more Christians understand the gospel, he says, the more they will be driven into this work.

A touch different from reading and retrieving a verse from James, isn't it?

When Christians realize that the gospel is central to the Christian mission and begin applying it to every aspect of life, perspectives and priorities radically change. The culture-warring Christian, for example, rushes off to fight the "war on Christmas" and force the employees at Target to quit saying, "Happy Holidays." A gospel-centered Christian says, "Christmas in America has very little to do with the incarnation of Christ anyway. Let's focus our energies on what's really important." The former believes we must forcibly change society to give us hope for a better future; the latter realizes that the only path to a better future runs through the good news of Jesus Christ.

Today's Christians have reflected on culture and have decided to stop separating from it, to stop outright condemning it and instead engage it. Their guide for how to engage the world— from their private lives to the public square—is the word of God seen through the prism of Jesus. And this leads them to live a life that proclaims and embodies the good news of this biblical Christ as they attempt to live life by the power of the gospel.

*   *   *

Nestled into the sheets of my "home office" that November, I thought of the rising generation's motivations in light of the

Manhattan Declaration. Turning to my computer, I penned an article for the *Washington Post*'s On Faith column titled "Manhattan Declaration Unlikely to Inspire Young Christians." Colson and the other drafters recognized the changes going on among the faithful but, I argued, they walked a poor path in their attempt to correct it.

Young Christians today don't want education on these issues; they want inspiration. They desire to be stirred by a strategy that addresses our world's many problems—not just a few of them. They wish for something that feels less like a series of logical arguments and meticulous talking points, and more like an invitation to live in the way of Jesus in a new age. They don't need another protest, but rather a promising vision for how the gospel might go forward in all of life, including the public square.

"Will the Manhattan Declaration inspire a new generation?" I asked in my column. Perhaps, but it doesn't seem likely. I respect many of the individuals whose names are affixed to the declaration, and I find many of their statements applause worthy. Yet, I suspect it will take more than a heady declaration from even such an august body of Christians to sway a new generation who take a broader view of cultural issues facing us today.

As Dan Gilgoff phrased it in his *God and Country* blog at *U.S. News and World Report*, "It's an interesting goal that says a lot about the fears of a graying generation of culture warriors, but the big question is how to instill the declaration's principles in the new generation. Releasing a 4,700-word document at the National Press Club doesn't seem like the straightest path to young people's hearts."[21]

The declaration garnered hundreds of thousands of signatures, but in the days since the release, it has never organically emerged in any conversation I've had with young Christian leaders. Older generations offer much wisdom from which we should learn, and new ideas from fresh voices can invigorate the learned. Younger Christians often make the mistake of parading around in our enlightened intelligence while older ones only stoop from their platforms and lecterns to educate us youngsters. Maybe the time has come to stop penning declarations that speak *at* each other and instead sit down at a table *with* each other where we can talk about the many issues our faith speaks to.[22]

This broken world needs us.

All of us.

EIGHT

A Touch Closer

Many people are good at talking about what they are doing, but in fact do little. Others do a lot but don't talk about it; they are the ones who make a community live.

—Jean Vanier

The Kolkata sun was just peeking over the horizon when I awoke. I'd been in India for a little more than four days, but my body was resisting the time change. Rolling onto my back, I stared into the barely visible ceiling of my room at the YMCA.

Paint peeling.

Muggy.

Mosquitoes.

After circling my head, one pest landed on my cheek and pricked my skin; my reticence to move almost convinced me to let him finish his breakfast. I begrudgingly swatted into the air, and as my insect wake-up call flew away, I rose to begin my day.

I was travelling with my friend Chris Heuertz, executive director of Word Made Flesh (WMF). WMF's mission is to serve Jesus among the poorest of the poor. From building orphanages for children with AIDS to rescuing women from the sex trade to ministering to people who are poor in South America's most destitute favelas, WMF pursues its mission in places that make most Americans cringe.

I had supported Chris and WMF in the past, but I wanted to do more than make a donation. I wanted to experience their mission firsthand. After months of prodding, Chris agreed to take me with him to Asia. Our 17-day trek landed us in two Indian states as well as Kathmandu, Nepal, and Bangkok, Thailand. This day, we were in the bustling city of Kolkata, where Chris arranged for me to serve in one of Mother Teresa's homes for the infirm and dying.

When Chris was at Asbury College in the 1990s, he felt a call on his life to serve the poor. He headed straight to India with almost no money in his pocket and ended up on Mother Teresa's doorstep. She took him in for a time, letting him work in her storied hospital. Chris spoke fondly of the woman he called "Mother," and his work there shaped his sense of vocation and understanding of the Christian call to justice and compassion.

On this particular day, I rose just after six to begin getting ready for my work. Because of water rationing, I was unable to take a shower—an inconvenience I now realize is normal for many Indians and much of the world's population. Luckily, I had filled two buckets with water—clean, but not potable—before going to bed the previous night. Stripping off my clothes, I squatted on the concrete floor and poured the frigid water over my naked body. My thoughts also washed over me, and I wondered what the ongoing work of the inevitable "Saint Teresa" would be like.

A WMF field director soon arrived in a dent-riddled taxicab, and we sped through the congested city of more than 15 million. Buildings of European architecture lined the streets—remnants of British colonialism, their colors faded by time and stained gray by smog. Arriving at the Missionaries of Charity convent around seven, I stopped by Mother Teresa's grave for a moment to pay my respects. Her simple white stone resting place aligned her death with her life—no extravagance, no decoration. After a few moments of quiet, I left to meet Sister Mercy, who registered me for service and sent me on my way.

A short bus ride later, I reached a massive facility in the middle of an endless landscape of crumbling houses constructed of sheet-metal shacks. Trash and the begging poor created a gauntlet of obstacles en route to the entrance. A sign atop the building read "Premdan," meaning "house of love."

As I entered, no one greeted me—no volunteer coordinator, no facility manager. There was too much important work to do. I froze, overwhelmed and unsure about where to begin. I walked over to the male ward, where volunteers scurried between patients, bandaging their wounds, shaving their faces, and cutting their hair. *This is what the Pool of Bethesda must have been like*, I thought as I wandered through a hoard of men, most of them lying on the ground in the courtyard, looking into the distance, never speaking. I couldn't imagine the physical and emotional pain these men must have felt; I coveted a knowledge of their thoughts.

My feet led me up the stairs of the men's housing unit, and the conditions worsened. Beds were strewn out on a grid throughout the expansive room. Emaciated bodies lay upon the sheets, and moans filled the air. I imagined that the aches of their illnesses worsened from their life's isolation. I stood motionless for several minutes.

Contemplating.

Processing.

"You sir," a man said, clasping my shoulder. "Come assist me."

From his accent, it was clear that the man was German. The ripples on his sun-scorched cheeks suggested he was about 80 years old.

Following him, I approached a patient lying next to the door whose foot was swollen to three or four times the normal size. The skin's green hue indicated it was probably gangrenous.

"He hasn't bathed in more than ten years," the German informed me. "The skin around his wound is like the scales of a fish and must be scrubbed before we can treat him. It's going to be very painful, and I'll need to hold him down."

He reached into his pocket and handed me a wire brush like the one I clean my grill with.

"Scrub," he barked, grasping the man's shoulders and pressing him into the wall against which he was leaning. "Scrub with all your strength!"

As soon as I began, the man started screaming. I pushed through his cries, continuing to force the bristles deep into his foot. Dead skin accumulated on the tops of my sandal-strapped feet and made piles between my toes. His skin bled in places, but the German continued to press me.

Despite my efforts to ignore them, the wails of the patient were impossible to block out.

"Please, Baba," the man begged me. "Please stop. Please."

"Baba" means father. The man thought I was a priest. Tears pooled in my eyes as I relentlessly scrubbed. Finally, we finished, and the German handed me a small jar of Vaseline and some toenail clippers.

"Now make him love you again," he said.

I rubbed the salve into the fresh skin on his foot before clipping his gnarled toenails. His breathing patterns returned to normal.

"Thank you, Baba."

I turned to depart, already looking for a place to slip away and have a good cry, but the German bellowed from across the room: "We have more work to do." I rushed to his side, where he was attending to a skeleton lying on his back. From what I could tell, every strand of muscle tissue on this man's bones was gone. Skin hung off his appendages like bat wings. His protruding hip bones looked like ball bearings.

We rubbed down the stick figure of a man with coconut oil and cream, being careful to mind the bedsores. The man groaned.

"Make him comfortable," the German instructed as he rose to walk away. "He will be gone before morning."

I continued to massage this man's body, lifting his sides to access his back. I stooped to pray in his ear as tears fell from my face to his pillow, but I knew not whether he could hear me. His jaw hung open and he stared into the air; his eyes were sunken and empty.

When I finished, I washed my hands and again joined the German, this time accepting my role as his assistant. No interview necessary—there wasn't time. For the next several hours we performed humiliating procedures for the infirm and dying.

Finally, a bell rang.

"It's time for tea," he said, tossing his gloves into a rusty trash can.

* * *

I took my time walking to the pavilion, hoping to stave off emotional shock. I entered the open space, took a plastic cup filled with black tea and milk, and joined the German, who was already resting under the shade of a tree. I felt like I needed to be alone, but this man had become my boss and my friend over the past several hours. I could at least offer him some worthwhile conversation.

Helmut had been coming to Premdan for ten years in six-month rotations. During this time, he had become something of a self-educated doctor, but in his pre-Kolkata days he'd been a Lutheran minister. I struggled to find something profound to ask this sage who'd experienced so much.

"Some great theologians have come from Germany over the years, huh?" I asked as a where-did-that-come-from look shot across my face.

He said he feared that the great days of the German church were past. Christian leaders in Germany were struggling with an increasingly secular society. They started focusing energy on petitioning politicians for institutional recognition. The church was now busy fighting with businesses and government, trying to pressure them to recognize its existence and its values. But along the way, he said, it had lost itself and lost sight of its mission.

"I suppose the German church and the American church are not so different as one might think," Helmut said.

"I suppose not."

He turned to me with a look that only an aged and experienced person can give. It was as if his eyes were prophesying, telling me to listen up because I was about to receive some great wisdom.

"Christians in America and Germany forget that it is not what you think or how much power you have or how you vote that changes the world. It's your hands that do the changing."

He wiggled his pruny digits.

"I held that man as you cleaned his feet. Did we change him? Perhaps. But he'll need to be cleaned again. I *do* know that he changed us," Helmut reflected. "In a small way, God worked through us and, as a result, this world moved just a touch closer to what He'd have it be.

"That's really why I'm here," he continued. "When I had my own congregation, I'd read Jesus' words in Matthew about being the salt of the earth, but I didn't fully understand it."

He turned to look out over the courtyard: "Now I know."

I sat in silence, stunned by the way this man summed up everything I'd been feeling. Helmut witnessed the church being led astray from her mission, seduced by power and lured by partisanship. He'd had a difficult time reconciling the teachings of Jesus with the actions of his church. Confused and spiritually hungry, he came to Mother Teresa's hospital, and there he found everything he'd been looking for: hope, inspiration, and answers. Helmut looked down again at the gnarled hands lying in his lap, and the bell rang for work to begin again.

• • •

In the days since leaving Premdan, I've held tightly to the experience so as not to forget. My time there is as fresh in my heart as when it happened. I keep seeing Helmut's hands in my mind, and I keep thinking about Jesus. I find myself weighing the old man's words against the stories of the Gospels—from healings to feedings, from Christ's life to His death and resurrection— and I think he's on to something.

Jesus didn't begin His ministry with a six-point agenda. Instead, He launched His public work with two simple words: "Follow me." And then He set out on a living lecture to illustrate to us what following Him looked like. He healed the sick and fed the hungry, worked miracles that still boggle modern minds. He preached the kingdom, promoted a new way of living, and then bore His cross to a hill called the place of the skull, where He offered His life as a sacrifice for all.

When religion squelches our childlike faith, we're driven back to Jesus' first words. When we feel alone in our spiritual journeys—those moments when we find ourselves staring into the stars and begging the Creator to speak to us—Jesus' words echo into our lives. "Follow me," our Savior says as He points to His footprints.

Jesus was hands-on. He was always touching people, playing with children, and rubbing His spit in other's eyes. He was present with those who needed Him, never content to let His disciples do the work for Him. If following Jesus means living like Christ did, then it must cost something.

Time.

Resources.

Vocation.

Even our lives.

Jesus' life was actually the key to His effectiveness. When He opened His mouth, He was a great teacher and His words melted the crowds. But there were countless good teachers in His days. What set Jesus a notch above them? The Scripture says that Christ left people slack-jawed "because he taught as one who had authority, and not as their teachers of the law."[1]

What could Matthew mean? Jesus was a rabbi, but He didn't have a synagogue. He was a teacher, but no school claimed Him. The difference is that Jesus didn't just prophesy from on high, promoting a list of rules and claiming to care about "issues." Jesus embodied everything He taught.

Jesus-followers can't flip through the browning pages of the Bible, reading about Christ's life and then go do something else—vote or mobilize or advocate. They can't rely on others to do their work. Christians must be present among those who need us, giving themselves to the needy and for the needy. Jesus' life stands in stark contrast to most culture-warring Christians. He didn't just advocate. He lived and dwelled and touched and healed.

The Apostle John was getting at this idea when he said, "That is how we know we are living in him. Those who say they live in God should live their lives as Jesus did."[2]

John speaks a word for us today here by saying, "If you claim to love who Jesus is, you should walk like Jesus did." Today, more than 2 billion people on planet Earth claim to follow Jesus, and I wonder how many of our lives look like His.

The formula for following Jesus is simple: Follow Jesus. Live like He did, give yourself to others, and share the good news that God has brought freedom to us all. Being faithful disciples of Christ in this century is no different than it was two millennia ago. If that's what Christians claim to be, they must make good on their professions of faith.

Is it enough to "advocate" for the hungry when we can satiate their hunger? Can we claim to follow Jesus if we do nothing ourselves for the poor He cared so much about? And what of the plight of orphans and the abandoned elderly? Does God let us off the hook when we ignore their problems except every fourth November? The more I press my feet into the steps Christ once trod, the more I hear Him calling away from an "advocacy only" religion to a "follow me" faith.

* * *

If the abortion debate were a retail store, the sign over the door might read "Dividing America Since 1973." That was the year of *Roe v. Wade*, a landmark Supreme Court case that legalized so-called abortion-on-demand in the United States. From that decision until today, abortion has been a bloody battleground for those fighting the culture wars.

Today, about 42 percent of Americans call themselves "pro-choice" and 51 percent call themselves "pro-life." We've reached an ideological stalemate,[3] and many of today's Christians have tired of the debate. The sound bites are worn out, the rhetoric is often devoid of basic civility, and despite the best Christian efforts, we've failed to induce much movement on the issue in the last 30 years.[4]

"Americans are tired of the rancor and name-calling. It has not only become non-productive, but it has almost become boring. People are not weary of the cause, but they are tired of the debate itself," says Joel Hunter, the pro-life pastor of Northland Church. "Since overturning *Roe v. Wade* is not realistic in the foreseeable future, if you're pro-life, you have to find different ways to combat abortion. I've always been a person that thinks that employing many methods toward the same goal is more effective than employing one method. Any progress we can make is still progress."[5]

Progress for Hunter involves using our collective time and resources to reduce the impetus for abortion in America. It means advocating for and providing aid for expectant mothers, increased access to contraception for low-income women, and greater incentives for adoption. This new angle on America's most vicious debate is being called the "abortion reduction" agenda, an idea that is resonating with individuals on both sides of the issue.

The breadth of supporters for the reduction agenda is impressive. Conservatives like Randy Brinson of Redeem the Vote and centrists like Richard Mouw of Fuller Theological Seminary support the agenda. Joining them are progressives like Jim Wallis of Sojourners and Rabbi David Saperstein of the Religious Action Center of Reform.

Not everyone is enthusiastic. Some all-or-nothing advocates from both the Right and the Left have responded with disdain. The founder of the Pro-Life Action League called abortion reduction a sellout and Douglas Johnson of the National Right to Life Committee said it was the burial ground for the pro-life movement.[6] Progressive writer Frank Clarkston claimed that the movement was rooted in anti-abortion tactics while Sarah Posner wrote in the *American Prospect* that it was "incrementalism masquerading as progressivism."[7]

Despite the naysayers, most Americans support efforts to reduce abortions. According to a 2008 poll by Public Religion Research, 83 percent of *all* voters agreed that elected leaders on both sides should work together to find ways to reduce the number of abortions by enacting policies that help prevent unintended pregnancies, expand adoption, and increase economic support for women who wish to carry their pregnancies to term. The poll found similar percentages among pro-life voters, white evangelicals, and Catholics.

The opportunity and the statistics beckon today's Christians to consider how they are living out their belief in the sanctity of human life. Will believers continue to just vote for pro-life candidates and let them bear the burden of this issue or will they take a cue from Jesus and enter this debate with their lives? Some Christians seem to be so deeply invested in the culture wars that they refuse to consider anything other than their status quo advocacy work. But following Jesus might require more from us. Much more.

The city where I live—Atlanta—is something of a Christian mecca. Megachurches (most of them evangelical Protestant congregations) dot the landscape, and nearly everyone claims to attend church somewhere. In a wealthy city like ours, the annual budgets of many churches are staggering. Within a ten-mile radius of my home you will find hundreds of houses of worship with budgets totaling in the tens of millions.

If you polled the members and ministers in these churches, you would find that most are unequivocally pro-life. But what are they doing about the "culture of death" in America? The pastor might preach a sermon about protecting the unborn on

"Sanctity of Life Sunday" or perhaps he'll introduce a local pro-life politician prior to the election. If you're lucky, the church might even support a pregnancy resource center.

I wonder how our community might be different if our churches banded together on this issue. What if we took all the money that pays for over-the-top programming or staff members whose jobs could and should be done by the congregants themselves[8] and placed it for practical use in reducing abortions?

"If you are a woman who feels like you cannot bring your child to term for any reason, come see us first," our collective of churches might declare. "We will walk beside you during this process to ensure that you can bring your child to term and provide for that child's needs in infancy. We will purchase the diapers and pay for the doctor visits. If you worry you can't provide for your child because you lack an education, we'll pay for your schooling. If you need to work and can't afford day care during your child's early years, we'll cover it."

How might the abortion debate look different in my community if that were our approach? Our commitment to an ethic of life would still be reflected in individual political advocacy and voting decisions, but our claims to love life would be made credible by our actions.

Following Jesus doesn't mean exiting the public square. Read the New Testament even once and you'll realize that following Jesus cannot be a private matter. Christians may often follow Jesus into the public square. Nineteenth-century Christian abolitionists did, and so did twentieth-century civil rights leaders. But they should never equate advocacy with followship as if they can vote their way into God's graces. The faithful must put feet to faith and engage their hands for the healing, helping, and restoration of this world.

In the words of John Stott, "While personal commitment to change our life-style without political action to change systems of injustice lacks effectiveness, political action without personal commitment lacks integrity."[9]

* * *

When Jesus walked among us, He was always showing up in unexpected places. In one of the gospel's most retold stories, Christ ended up staying with a man named Simon in Bethany. This is astonishing because Simon either was a leper or had been one in the past. But it didn't matter to Jesus. He preferred the company of unclean outcasts. And in the home of this pariah, the most amazing story unfolds.

At a dinner given in Jesus' honor, Martha was serving the guests while Lazarus and others reclined at the table with Jesus. In a shocking act, Mary took a pint of expensive perfume, poured it on Jesus' feet, and wiped His feet with her hair. At this, the Scriptures say, the entire house filled with the fragrance. The rest of the dinner guests were enraged. They couldn't believe she had wasted this perfume—worth an entire year's wages—in such a way. Mary didn't care what they thought; she knew that the value of the person who sat before her was infinitely greater than the liquid in her bottle. She emptied it on Jesus with joy, and He defended her decision, asking the others to leave her alone.[10]

In the story's background, another woman named "Martha" lingers. The Scripture simply says she served, but no reading of the text leaves her a hero in the story. Standing in repose where she stirred stew or baked bread, Martha rarely came into contact with Jesus Himself. She was following her "checklist" and carrying out her agenda, but she missed the great opportunity before her to sit at the feet of the Son of God and lavish Him with her love as did her sister Mary.

We know that Martha's behavior is typical for her. In the Gospel of Luke, we meet her in a similar story, only this time dinner was being served in her home. Mary was there again as well and, as you might expect, was sitting like a dry sponge at the feet of the Lord soaking up every word He spoke. Martha was in the kitchen, and Luke says she was "distracted by all the preparations that had to be made." As the bread rose in the oven, so her anger swelled at being left alone to do all the cooking. In a fit of anger, Martha petitioned Jesus to make Mary come and help her in the kitchen.

"Martha, Martha," the Lord answered, "you are worried and upset about many things, but few things are needed—or indeed only one. Mary has chosen what is better, and it will not be taken away from her."[11]

When I read this story and think back over my life, I'd like to pretend that I'm Mary. But I'm not. I'm a Martha through and through. If I'm honest, the items on my worried-and-upset list range from the moral decline of America to how much money I'm paying in taxes. I've busied myself with these things— blogging about them, arguing about them, voting for them. I've allowed myself to get so caught up in the culture-war kitchen serving up judgment for all who don't join my cause that I've missed the better choice.

I envision Jesus turning to Martha, turning to me, and letting out a disappointed sigh.

"I appreciate all the good work you're doing," He might say. "But don't get so swept up in it that you lose sight of the most important thing—following me in service to others."

Reading over the pages that bear this narrative, a quiet, inconspicuous word shouts out to me: *fragrance*. More than a physical element in this story, the aroma from Mary's flask gives us a picture of Christ Himself. When we choose to sit at the feet of our Lord and break open the bottle of our lives in service to Him, His fragrance fills the world.

The Apostle Paul's second letter to the Corinthians echoes this story: "But thanks be to God, who in Christ always leads us in triumphal procession, and *through us spreads the fragrance* of the knowledge of him everywhere."[12]

This is what happened in the leper's house that day. Everyone wanted to eat with Christ and claim Him as their friend. Only one was willing to abandon the table and sit at His feet, to offer a gift worthy of the guest of honor, to release the scent of sacrifice. Mary's act illustrates a timeless lesson: when we are broken for Christ, we release His essence to the world.[13]

This is the call of Jesus on our lives—to be broken for Him, to live lives of sacrificial followship so that His fragrance may expand. It must cost us something; it must involve a breaking. No cheap or easy advocacy can fully answer this call. In the end, our beliefs, our love, our "values" cannot be simply voted. They must be embodied.

The more I observe a new generation of Christians, the more I sense that they don't want to be diverted from our gospel-focused, Christ-centered mission in pursuit of other goals, even good ones. They hear Jesus instruct them:

- "Don't be fooled into thinking you can build my kingdom by simply manipulating the systems of this world. Declare and embody the good news, and I will reign."
- "Seek not earthly power in this world. If you want to be first, strive to be last. Serve others, and exalt me."
- "Resist the lure of partisanship and its promise of communal advancement. Become my servant, and you will be a servant to all."
- "Remain faithful in all matters and in all places—yes, even the public square. But do not desire to sit at the tables of those you think 'great.' Sit at my feet instead. Break your life open for me and for others, and I will fill your house with my fragrance."

Today's Christians are making a positive course correction by moving beyond partisan politics, by following Jesus without fighting the culture wars. You might say the change we're witnessing is a shift from a political faith to an incarnational faith. One that seeks to be a faithful presence in the public square but knows that real change happens when we heal and help each other.

The call of Jesus is ultimately not a call to productive citizenship, but an invitation to leave everything and follow a new king. Today's Christians don't want to get so hot in pursuit of political goals that they stop chasing after Jesus. So they no longer see the public square as a means to achieve power. God has already given Christians all the power they need. They will no longer allow partisanship to divide the church. Nothing should separate what God has joined together. They are beating their culture-warring swords into kingdom plowshares, and I believe they'll be better for it.

A hospital is filled to overflowing with the sick and dying in Kolkata, India. And in Russia. And China. And Nigeria. They are waiting for the good news of Jesus to be declared and embodied. And I have a feeling that more than a few here in America—the broken, the abused, the outcast, the poor—need the same. Like Helmut, may we engage our hands for Jesus through service and sacrifice for others. And like Mary, may we sit at Jesus' feet and through our brokenness release His sweet fragrance into the world.

NINE

One Hundred Pianos

*If Christians cannot extend grace through faithful
presence within the body of believers, they will not be
able to extend grace to those outside.*

—JAMES DAVISON HUNTER

I attended the most amazing church this morning, and it was
my own.

Fewer Christians are saying that these days, I'm finding. Either
the pastor is too boring or the people seem too perfect or the
service runs too long or the music is too traditional or too contemporary or too loud or too unfamiliar. So many people shop
around for a place to belong like bargain hunters in pursuit of
the best sale ever. But for many Christians the concerns run
deeper than aesthetics and sermon content. Christ-followers of
all ages are questioning whether the church—the Bride of
Christ—is overlooking its mission and growing too devoted to
its own self-survival. Many regular church attenders are
demanding answers from the universal fellowship of believers.

One might expect our faith to be attacked and scrutinized
from the outside by those like the late Christopher Hitchens

and Richard Dawkins. But critical voices are crying out from within the church. They are perhaps epitomized most popularly by Rob Bell, who compares the church to a velvet-adorned painting of Elvis that he owns—earnest but kitschy, a token from another era.[1] I hear perspectives like this frequently.

Call me strange, but I love my church—despite her failings and flaws, of which there are many—and I feel privileged to be a part of it.

While I was still in high school, my dad told me he was dreaming about starting another campus of our current church or perhaps a new church altogether. God had nurtured a holy discontent within my dad's heart for many years. He loved his congregation, but he recognized that we were not reaching whole swaths of our community—from young people to those of color. God was nurturing in him a vision for a space where worshipers could engage God without having to step over the cultural baggage you'd encounter in many evangelical congregations. A place to which we wouldn't be afraid or embarrassed to invite friends who didn't look, think, behave, vote, or believe as we did. A church that, while holding fast to the gospel, would build bridges of connection rather than construct walls of division.

Even as this vision welled up inside Dad, the ease of his job gave him pause. He had pastored our previous church for 18 years, and life was comfortable for us. The church was thriving, and the people loved our family deeply. At the same time, this nearly 125-year-old congregation was steeped in tradition and might not follow him across such an unfamiliar bridge. If he followed the vision God gave him, he'd risk losing something he loved dearly.

A breaking point came when my younger brother confessed, "Dad, if you weren't pastoring this church, I wouldn't attend here." Hearing this from one of his own children pushed him over the edge, and he decided to move forward.

When I first heard Dad share his heart, the high school version of me only pretended to listen—I wasn't too interested in such matters at the time—but I remember the firestorm of passion that flashed through his eyes as he explained what he believed God was calling him to do. Four years later, in 2003, his dream came true, and Cross Pointe Church was born.

We started with a handful of members, but they were faithful in giving and serving. Talented ministers took pay cuts to come join us in the work. And thanks to a generous donation, we moved into a permanent location in less than one year. We converted an old Boeing manufacturing plant, where the cruise missiles for the first Gulf War had been constructed, into our worship center and offices. Two models of missiles had been built there—employees had nicknamed them "hellfire" and "damnation." God must indeed have a sense of humor.

Each time I drive onto campus and see our buildings, I remember the prophet Isaiah's picture of the kingdom of God: "They will beat their swords into plowshares and their spears into pruning hooks." A facility that was once used to make war is now a place of worship and ministry.

God has granted Cross Pointe many successes throughout the years, but we've also encountered numerous frustrations, challenges, and setbacks. We've weathered lean years and tough times. We look back and recognize mistakes we made and problems we let linger too long. Planting our church was not easy, as might be assumed, but the blessings of our community far outweigh the burdens.

Perhaps the most surprising gift God has given our church is diversity. Our previous church was a stereotypical white Southern Baptist congregation—a homogenous collection of conservative, lifelong Baptists. Cross Pointe, however, is a kaleidoscope of races, political perspectives, and faith traditions.

Approximately one-third of our congregation is made up of people of color, and that number is growing steadily. On a given Sunday at Cross Pointe, you'll encounter Indian Americans in full saris, African Americans, and first- and second-generation Asians and Latin Americans for whom English is not their primary language.

This morning during our service, I sat near the front and enjoyed the wonderful friends who sat around me. To my right was a Pentecostal woman who lifts her hands when she sings and to my left was a reserved Korean couple, raised Presbyterian. Just in front of me were two of our most precious members, both of whom were raised in predominantly Hindu communities in India but now follow Christ. And next to them sat a newly married couple, one formerly Catholic and one previously agnostic.

Such diversity is surprising if you know much about our community. Forsyth County, just a few miles from where our church sits, once gained a national audience for its blatant racism. In 1987, when the *Oprah Winfrey Show* had been on the air for a mere six months, the daytime diva brought her cameras to a city in Forsyth for a town hall meeting. At the time, not even one black person resided there. In the meeting, several residents spoke out against a mixed-race community and defended their right to keep their city ethnically "pure."[2]

Just a few miles from where Oprah's now infamous show was filmed a mere 25 years ago, I found myself worshiping alongside a rainbow of races, and my heart was light. I recalled the Apostle John's picture in Revelation 5:9 of the crowd gathered "from every tribe and language and people and nation" who join together in singing a new song.

The people of Cross Pointe also display great political diversity. During a Sunday service just before the 2008 presidential election, I walked our church parking lot and was surprised and delighted to encounter vehicles adorned with both McCain-Palin and Obama-Biden bumper stickers (and even a lonely window cling for the Libertarian Party candidate). Pick an issue—health care, taxes, welfare—and you'll find church members on both sides.

Yet all of these individuals drive onto the same campus to be a part of our loving community without fear of alienation. We keep partisan politics out of our pulpit and our programming. We don't pass out voter's guides, and Dad doesn't publicly endorse candidates. We're a far cry from the church that allowed partisanship to creep in on Sundays, the church in which President Clinton was called an "idiot" and no one bristled. All are welcome at Cross Pointe regardless of their political views or party affiliation.

Our members could tell you that we aren't a perfect church, but I believe we're moving closer to the church God wants us to be. Each person standing around me has come from a different community and culture, but somehow we sing with one voice, worship the same risen Lord together. I'm satisfied with this church that God has built, but I also realize that it wouldn't be possible if Cross Pointe were entrenched in America's culture wars.

*   *   *

The culture wars, like all wars, seek to divide. They pronounce our differences rather than celebrate them. They highlight disagreement instead of common ground. They force us to see brothers and sisters as enemies rather than friends with whom we may disagree. Where the culture wars are fought, unity is almost always absent.

In the past few years, I've spoken in dozens of churches across the country that span the spectrum from liberal to conservative. And the damaging effects of the culture wars are often painfully apparent. Often I'm asked to share what the Bible says about caring for creation. When addressing this sensitive subject, I always root myself in what the Scriptures actually say. I avoid such contentious issues as the claims of climate science, and I never wade into debates about specific legislative proposals. I stick to the Bible's witness on the subject and attempt to give listeners a framework in which they can begin thinking about these issues for themselves. The quotes I use come from figures like Martin Luther and Billy Graham. I've been blessed to see many Christians on both sides of the issue disarmed by these talks.

Yet, some people who assume that a biblical message *must* be political get angry and begin to label me before I even open my mouth. Sometimes in more liberal churches, I'm asked why I don't take a harder stance on certain issues or why I don't devote more time to calling out conservatives who ignore the Bible's call to care for creation. After giving talks at more conservative churches, I'm often accosted by people who assume I'm advocating for extreme environmental policies or attempting to diminish the Creator at the expense of the creation. These individuals often label me a socialist or earth-worshiper or pagan, and one blogger even encouraged people on his website to "please pray for this young man. He needs salvation and his message is poison."

Authors Shane Claiborne and Jonathan Wilson-Hartgrove witnessed similar divisions when engaging the issue of poverty. They noted that the church, which should be unified in its love for and support of the poor, has been held captive by the world's debates over the issue. Christians on the right argued that the best way to reduce poverty was to encourage capitalistic growth through tax breaks, while Christians on the left countered that we needed more taxes for government programs that assist people's basic needs and work to alleviate the causes of poverty.

"We're not sure who's right, but we have noticed that the debates don't seem to do much for the people in our neighborhoods," Claiborne and Wilson-Hartgrove write. "What it does, unfortunately, is divide the church. Christians seem to feel more allegiance to the political right or left than we feel to God's people. Rather than share what we have in common so that no one has need, we self-segregate into conservative and liberal congregations or black and white congregations or upper- and lower-class congregations."[3]

Deep divisions exist in the church today as a result of poor theology, political partisanship, and uncivil rhetoric.

• • •

When the American church enlists in the culture wars, it ceases to be either fully "American" or fully "the church." Our citizens have always fought over what their country should look like. Early American colonists tarred and feathered disagreeable Tories, and fistfights in the Senate chamber were not uncommon in the months leading up to the Civil War. Then there was the Civil War itself.

According to James Madison, we all owe our country "loving criticism." But the vision for Americans has been that we remain together in pursuit of our common goals even though we differ. A 1782 Act of Congress adopted *e pluribus unum* as the dictum on the Seal of the United States. The Latin phrase translates "out of many, one." When expressing the spirit of our heritage—the spirit of *e pluribus unum*—Americans are able to disagree with passion and civility, retaining the bonds of our common humanity and citizenry.

Christ's vision for His church actually sounds a lot like this. Jesus prayed in the Gospel of John, "Holy Father, protect them by the power of your name, the name you gave me, so that they may be one as we are one."[4] Christians are a community brought together by God the Father, His Son Jesus Christ, and the Holy Spirit, and what God has unified, humans should not seek to divide. They are bound together by one gospel and one mission and, though Christians fight the same fight, their struggle is not against each other.[5] Imagine how grieved Jesus, who prayed for unity, must be now as He looks at His fractured followers.

A. W. Tozer once noted that 100 pianos all tuned to the same fork are thereby tuned to one another. They find unity to each other, he says, by finding another standard to which each one must bow. Tozer saw in these theoretical pianos a powerful metaphor for the church: "So one hundred worshippers meeting together, each one looking away to Christ, are in heart nearer to each other than they could possibly be were they to become 'unity' conscious and turn their eyes away from God to strive for closer fellowship."[6]

Christians are not ultimately bound together by our political views or even the theological minutiae that splinter churches. The great unifier that draws us together is our common commitment to Jesus. He is the foundation of the faith, our ultimate hope, the reason we live. American Christians should strive for Jesus, knowing that through that effort unity will be achieved. We should not seek unity for the sake of unity, but because we follow Jesus. Those who realize this great truth become an ensemble of far more than 100 pianos playing together an irresistible score.

* * *

As we strive toward unity and imagine what the future might hold for the American church and our public witness, we cannot escape the issue of race.[7] The history of the American Christian movement on the issue of race, well, in the words of

Anne Lamott, "It's enough to make Jesus drink gin straight out of the cat dish."[8] My own denomination, the Southern Baptist Convention, was formed in 1845 over slavery. The first SBC churches were birthed out of a desire to appoint slaveholders as missionaries.[9]

Sadly, the tradition continued into the twentieth century as debates over segregation raged. Southern Baptist preachers vocally opposed the civil rights movement and supported Jim Crow laws.

In the 1950s, the *Alabama Baptist* newspaper editorialized, "We think it deplorable in the sight of God that there should be any change in the difference and variety in his creation and he certainly would desire to keep our races pure."[10] In 1956, Texas pastor W. A. Criswell, still considered a paragon among contemporary Southern Baptists, argued before a joint session of the South Carolina legislature that desegregation was un-Christian.

Contemporary white Christians often brush aside our history on the issues of slavery and segregation, but our heritage is a sobering reminder of the Christian tendency to manipulate the Scriptures in pursuit of political goals.

Criswell went on to apologize for that position, and the SBC passed a "Resolution on Racism" in 1989 asserting what might be the greatest denominational understatement of the last century: "Southern Baptists have not always clearly stood for racial justice and equality." Not surprisingly, African American Baptists formed their own congregations and affiliations; few are among our ranks today.

During the civil rights movement, opposition to integration was one of the primary smelling salts that awakened modern Christian political leaders out of their slumber.[11] By the 1970s, America's high courts, politicians, and theologians had settled the issue of segregation in principle. But a sect of America's religious leaders continued to resist the practical changes, arguing that integration was a demonic scheme to overthrow God's established order in favor of socialistic, dictatorial governance.[12] Many Southern Baptist Christians embraced such antiquated, uninformed thinking just a few decades ago, and the policies supported today by our lobbying arm on many issues often vary from those supported by many Christians of various ethnic backgrounds.

Old paradigms die hard. Even Christian publishing falls into this trap, often innocently and without malice, but still hurtful to the world around us. A few years ago, a Christian publisher released a book equating a particular ethnicity to character flaws. Another produced an Asian-themed Vacation Bible School curriculum that drew heavily on stereotypes, including chopsticks, karate uniforms, takeout boxes, and rickshaws.[13] The materials were distributed to an estimated 20,000 American churches.

When church leaders speak about race carelessly and when Christian products perpetuate racial stereotypes, encounters like this one from a blog post by an Asian American Christian are the result. A young man recounts a recent experience in his Missouri church. During the service, a non-Asian elder's wife dressed in a Japanese-style kimono stood at the front of the church to make an announcement about a new outreach program for international students. As she spoke in broken

English, attempting to fake an Asian accent, the congregation burst into raucous laughter.

He wrote:

> There were two Asians in church that day. One was me. The other was my unchurched friend. He turned to me and said, "this is bullsh-t." He got up, turned around (we were sitting in the front row) and walked past the crowd of 800 laughing and guffawing faces. To my knowledge, he has never stepped into a church again.[14]

Today, our world looks a lot different than it did in the 1950s, or even the 1980s. In the latter half of the twentieth century, approximately 22 million immigrants and between 7 and 10 million undocumented workers came to the United States.[15] Recent projections indicate that by 2050, our country will lack an ethnic majority.[16] America, and by default American churches, must move swiftly toward a multiethnic reality. Christians must begin including and validating diverse voices within our communities.

This is relevant for a discussion on faith and politics because Christians of color interact differently with the public square than do white Christians. African American Christians' perspectives are born out of the African American experience, just as the perspectives of Latin American Christians and Asian American Christians are born of their experiences. They may align politically in different ways than white Christians. They may express unique views on issues such as affirmative action, education, immigration, poverty, and systemic injustices. When believers speak imprudently or uncivilly about such issues or claim that God has an official policy position—which He does not—they alienate their Christian brothers and sisters unnecessarily.

As Christians contemplate the new racial reality in light of Revelation 5:9, we must begin constructing bridges across racial, religious, and political divides. I am not attempting to oversimplify this complex issue. But Christians must recognize that for all the progress made on many fronts, the issue of race continues to plague us.[17] We cannot have both liberation and domination, independence and exploitation, redemption and oppression, love and hatred. If ever the Christian community is to improve its public witness, it must concurrently overcome its failings on race—past and present.

*   *   *

The longer I live, the more I realize that anything worth doing is difficult. Dad also recognized this when he embarked on the great adventure of church planting. With each minor decision about how the new church would function, someone seemed disgruntled. Most of this feedback came from our Christian friends outside of our new congregation; they worried that we were moving too far from traditionalism.

One of the most controversial decisions made was the church's name. We realized that in our community, the word "Baptist" might be a barrier rather than a bridge. We were proud of our heritage, but we recognized those elements that were off-putting or even painful to those we wanted to reach. We were most focused on what we could do to draw our community, to be a church where even our name illustrated that all are welcome.

When we announced the church's name, "Cross Pointe Church," some of our Baptist friends were outraged. The nicer ones expressed confusion, and the bolder ones told us we were selling out. Many of these individuals were longtime friends who we spoke to weekly and who stayed in our home when they passed through town. Some of them haven't spoken to us since.

Dad never doubted that he was following God's will, but the weight of strained relationships weighed heavily on his heart. One day, Dad was in his library in the basement of his home when he broke down in tears under the pressure. He lay down on the floor with his face burrowed into the carpet, and cried out to God. As he prayed, he sensed God asking him a simple but profound question: "Do you trust Me?"

The question startled him, and then he heard it again: "Do you trust Me?"

Dad realized that doing a new work and challenging convention is difficult, but he could trust God to help him handle the difficulties. God didn't promise that achieving his vision would be easy, but Dad knew that God would weather the storms with him. He got up off the floor and went back to work.

As I observe the changing landscape of America, I'm struck by the great opportunities before us. I see the opportunity to change lives and shape them. I see the opportunity to influence the culture and the people who shape the culture. I recognize the opportunity to push the gospel of Jesus Christ forward like never before in a world where world travel is effortless and where we possess a gamut of technological tools unimagined even a generation ago. I see an occasion to eliminate extreme poverty, to bring basic needs like food and water to people who lack them, to set free those stuck in the slave trade, to beat back our culture of abortion, to fight debilitating diseases like AIDS, to place millions of orphans in loving homes, to stop making war and start making peace. I see a world where Christians work with each other, rather than against each other, to achieve these goals through the actions of individual believers working in the public square and churches mobilizing their people to get their hands dirty. I envision a church that trusts God so much that it's unified despite our differences, and a world that stands watching, slack-jawed by our accord.

TEN

The Burden of Every Generation

Each generation imagines itself to be more intelligent than the one that went before it, and wiser than the one that comes after it.

—GEORGE ORWELL

Seminary students are notoriously poor, and I was no exception. To make ends meet, I worked long days as a cell phone salesman. Sounds boring, I know, but I was pretty good at it and found it enjoyable. Slow sales days were grating, but fast ones were frantic and made up for the slower ones. One particular slow day, however, was as frantic as any fast day I can recall.

I sat at my desk staring at the empty parking lot through the glass door crowded with advertisements. The clicking of the clock above my head threatened to lull me to sleep. With each tock or tick, my eyelids opened a little less wide. And then right before my head slumped, my cell phone buzzed in my pocket.

I snapped awake. It was my dad.

"Son, a great man died today," he said as his voice broke. "Dr. Falwell has passed away."

The shock on my face would have been apparent had any customers been around to witness it.

"Are you there, Son?"

"Yes. I'm just stunned and don't know what to say."

Despite his faults and foibles, Falwell was a fixture in the evangelical world. Though he'd battled some health problems, I assumed he would always be around. Like Coca-Cola or Times Square. Dr. Falwell seemed indestructible. Fellow Liberty students and I used to joke that he'd outlive us all.

Dad and I were silent on the line for what felt like several minutes.

"I hope you'll come to the funeral with your mom and me," he finally said.

Though I've been critical of Dr. Falwell from time to time, I've always felt toward him a frustrated affection. His regular blunders created much tension between my non-Christian friends and me. Yet his kindness and generosity to me over the years could not go unthanked.

"I'll be there," I said.

When I entered the worship center at Thomas Road Baptist Church, I was flooded with a mixture of sadness and nostalgia. The sanctuary wasn't full, and despite the rumors, few prominent figures showed up for the service. No Sean Hannity, no Pat Robertson, no Reagan or Bush White House staffers. Those who needed him while he was alive forgot him quickly after his death. The only noteworthy attendees were a few "Christian celebrities." Televangelist Rod Parsley, Gary Bauer of American Values, and a couple members of the defunct musical group DC Talk were there to pay their respects, but I can remember few other notables.

The service was brief, and my tears surprised me. Dr. Falwell's passing was bigger than one man. He represented a way of being Christian, one that was quickly passing, in many ways. The slide show on the video screens pictured robed choirs and snippets from revivalist sermons. Memories from childhood and adolescence overwhelmed me. The tears flowed because I was saying good-bye to a piece of my past.

The casket was taken to the grave on Liberty's campus, but few outside of family were allowed to attend the burial. I drove my parents back to the Lynchburg, Virginia, airport as we reminisced about some of our fonder memories of his life, and then I began my drive home.

As my car cut through the foothills of the Blue Ridge Mountains, I pondered Jerry Falwell's life as I have on many days since we first sat to dine in the Lynchburg IHOP. This time, I wondered how Dr. Falwell saw his life from the other side of eternity. *Which decisions have been vindicated from beyond the grave, and which ones does he now realize were mistakes?*

When Richard Mouw, now the president of Fuller Theological Seminary, was a PhD student at the University of Chicago in 1967, he received a phone call from Carl Henry, editor of the newly launched *Christianity Today*. He had read an essay Mouw had written on social ethics and was impressed by his persuasive argumentation. He wanted to publish it, but with one "minor revision."

Mouw argued that *the church* should take stands on specific issues of social justice, but Henry wanted to change the wording to speak of *individual Christians* needing to take stands. But Mouw's original wording was intentional. He believed that the church as an institution should speak to specific social justice concerns in the public square, so he turned down Henry's offer.

Over the next two weeks, Henry suggested a number of wording compromises until he convinced a begrudging Mouw to let *Christianity Today* run the essay. The final version asserted that the church must maintain its prophetic voice and say "no" to the status quo of injustices, but stopped short of saying the church should endorse specific policy solutions.

Over the years, Richard Mouw spoke little about the essay and the exchange with Henry. More than four decades later, after Carl Henry passed away, however, Mouw sat down to pen another essay for the same publication.

"What I really wanted to say is that the church—in the form of both preaching and ecclesial pronouncements—could do more than merely utter a 'no' to some social evils," Mouw said. "There were times, I was convinced, that the church could rightly say a bold 'yes' to specific policy-like solutions. I now see that youthful conviction as misguided. *Henry was right, and I was wrong.*"[1]

This seasoned theologian came to see in his later years the wisdom of the ideas that Henry pioneered. Carl Henry believed that the *institutional church* has no authority, mandate, or competence to endorse specific legislation, military tactics, or economic proposals. But *individual Christians*, like all citizens, should engage these solutions to their "limit of competence and opportunity."[2] Of course, Henry would often add that there might arise "emergency situations," as in the case of Nazi Germany or slavery, when the church might receive a clear word from God to engage in a more concerted way. Without such a word, churches should continue to help their people think and act Christianly.

The church is historically at our worst when bogged down in policy debates and partisan squabbles. We're at our best when focused on the proclamation of the good news of Jesus, loving our neighbors, and providing a framework through which Christian people might make informed decisions.[3] As a good pastor friend said to me, "I never have to tell my people how to vote or which policies to support. If I'm discipling my people like I ought to be, I pretty much know how they'll come down."

With Liberty University well out of sight and my radio fading cyclically in and out of reception, I wondered if a postmortem Jerry Falwell looks more like the youthful Richard Mouw or the elder one.

It wasn't until many months after the funeral that I visited Jerry Falwell's burial site. My younger brother was now a student at Liberty, and I went to visit him. Picking him up and heading to dinner, the university campus came into view. Against my hungry brother's pleas, I made a last-minute decision to hit the off-ramp.

My car passed between the dogwood trees that line the main road and pulled up beside the oldest building on Liberty's campus, the Carter Glass Mansion. The 1923 stone home is named after its original owner, who was secretary of the treasury under President Woodrow Wilson. Sitting atop a grassy knoll overlooking the cafeteria and baseball stadium, "the mansion," as students call it, was the perfect place to bury the preacher. It housed the offices of the highest-ranking staff, including the one where Falwell worked to build his university and the Moral Majority. The same office where Falwell was found dead.

The grave site was modest. There was a stone tomb encircled by a small pool with an erect white cross no taller than I. An eternal flame burned atop the cross that, unlike Falwell, unlike us all, would live more than a lifetime.

History judges every prominent leader's legacy only after years of reflection. Looking down at this controversial man's final resting place, I began contemplating what his legacy might be. *How would people remember Jerry Falwell? As a soldier who fought for what he believed was right or more like a pied piper who led a sizeable chunk of American Christians into the culture wars?*

I believe Jerry Falwell was a good man, perhaps even a great man. He was a remarkable leader with an uncanny ability to energize a constituency. And he was a committed family man. A few years before he passed away, Dr. Falwell remarked that his family was his greatest accomplishment.[4] He was generous to a fault, and his belief that everyone deserves a chance at higher learning whether they could afford it or not got Liberty into financial trouble more than once. I'm a living testament to his openhandedness, as he provided me with a college education for which I will be forever grateful.

Most people remember his political organizing and gaffes, but Dr. Falwell accomplished much good that never made the news. Across from Liberty is a home he built for pregnant mothers who need support to bring their children to term. Not far from there, he built a recovery center for men who are alcoholics. Jerry Falwell cared about people. I will never forget the day I graduated, when he handed me my diploma and leaned in to hug and kiss me with genuine pride and affection.

One religion writer correctly opined after his passing, "Surely, the Rev. Falwell was a cracked vessel for the Spirit of God, but aren't we all."[5]

Sadly, the iconic evangelical preacher will be remembered more for his cracks than his many noble achievements.

Jerry Falwell's legacy will be conflicted, I think. As will the legacy of the late-twentieth-century Christian political movement in which he was a leader.

Yet we must not be so naïve as to think that the legacy of today's Christians will be any cleaner, any clearer. No generation is waterproof, soundproof, bulletproof, and untainted by our own fallenness. Just because my generation cannot yet see our blind spots doesn't mean they aren't there. We will, no, we *are* making grave mistakes. Different ones perhaps, but mistakes nonetheless.

And the generation that is yet to come will criticize us as we've criticized those before us. This is the burden of every generation. But we're also given an opportunity to build on those who came before us. We can only hope to learn enough from those who preceded us to avoid the greatest temptations and muster enough courage to solve a few problems along the way.

The sun was just beginning to scatter its dusky beams across the horizon, and I realized we were going to be late for dinner. As I turned to leave, I noticed the pensive look on my brother's face as he stood next to me and stared down at the grave.

"How do you think people will remember him?" he asked.

"I don't know," I said, turning to walk away. "If we aren't careful, probably a lot like they'll remember us."

Acknowledgments

You hold in your hands the work of a community, not an individual. I must thank everyone whose time and efforts breathed life into this project and shaped the one that penned it.

First of all, I'm so grateful to Jesus Christ. Thanking God in an acknowledgment section (or an end zone) is cliché these days, but I couldn't do what I do without my Lord. Jesus, you sustain me when I want to quit, and your life and teachings provide a constant well of wisdom in my life.

Thanks to my family, who continually supports me. To my dad, who is never afraid to challenge my thinking. Despite our occasional disagreement, we're better friends than we've ever been. You are a sharpening iron in my life. To my mom, who reads everything I write and anchors me with her gentle, motherly insights. To my brothers, who keep me humble by constantly reminding me that I'm not "some big-shot writer" and then let me know that they're proud of me. Also, thanks to my grandmother, Mim, who prays over my life every single day.

To my mentor and friend, Margaret Feinberg. You push me to remain a writer of excellence and integrity and never balk when I need a swift kick of honesty. This book exists, in large part, because of you.

Thanks to the editor on this project, Adrienne Ingrum. Truth be told, you probably deserve as much credit for this book as I do. You urged me to keep going when I was running out of gas, and you shaped the content through your passionate attention to detail. I've never worked with such a wonderful editor, and I hope this is not our last project together.

Thanks to the entire FaithWords team—especially Joey Paul, Shanon Stowe, Jana Burson, and Harry Helm. Working with a team like this is a writer's dream and a lot of fun to boot. Also, thanks to Kelly Hughes of Dechant-Hughes, who masterfully spearheaded the public relations effort for this book as she did for the last.

Thanks to Erik Wolgemuth and the whole team at Wolgemuth and Associates, who believed in this book and offered wisdom that helped shape it.

Thank you to Chris Ferebee for working so hard to see this project through. I look forward to working together on compelling projects for a long time.

To all those friends who have come alongside me in the past few years to offer encouragement and criticism in the confines of friendship: Jason Locy, Tim Willard, Tyler Wigg-Stevenson, Danny Akin, Gabe Lyons, David Gushee, Ken Coleman, Joel Hunter, Rusty Pritchard, Steve Monsma, Dean Inserra, Brent Cole, Byron Borger, Ben Ortlip, Tom Krattenmaker, Ron Sider, Johnny Carr, Chris Heuertz.

To all those who offered invaluable feedback that made this book so much stronger: Sarah Baik, Lindsie Yancey, Barry

Hankins, Steven Monsma, Maegan Carberry, Byron Borger Clayton Shaw, Mandy Anderson, Melissa Brown, Adam Scott Greenwald, Addison Nieman, Logan McElroy.

Finally, thanks to all my editors over the years who gave me the space to work out my thoughts in columns and articles throughout their publications. I especially thank Roxy Wiemann, Ryan Hamm, Elizabeth Tenety, John Siniff, Cricket Fuller, Scott Marshall, Lindy Lowry, Ken Foskett, and Dan Gilgoff.

To all I've forgotten, grace and gratitude.

About the Author

Jonathan is a faith and culture writer who has published over three hundred articles in respected outlets such as *USA Today*, the *Atlanta Journal-Constitution*, the *Christian Science Monitor*, *Beliefnet*, *CNN.com*, *Christianity Today*, and the *Washington Post*'s On Faith column. His first book, *Green Like God: Unlocking the Divine Plan for Our Planet*, was called "mandatory reading for churchgoers" by *Publishers Weekly*. As a respected Christian voice, Jonathan has been interviewed by ABC World News, CNN, Fox News, NPR, PBS, CBS Radio, the *New York Times*, and *Slate.com*.

Jonathan first entered the public eye when a classroom epiphany prompted him to organize a national coalition of Christian leaders who care about creation, founding the Southern Baptist Environment and Climate Initiative. Since then, he's been on the front lines of pressing cultural conversations from poverty to orphan care. He is a member of the national board of directors for Bethany Christian Services, America's largest adoption agency. Because of his work, *Outreach* magazine recently named him one of "30 Emerging Influencers" reshaping twenty-first-century Christian leadership.

Known for his ability to tackle difficult issues through both the written and the spoken word, Jonathan has become a sought-after speaker by colleges, seminaries, churches, and conferences on cultural and religious issues. He holds a master of divinity from Southeastern Baptist Theological Seminary and a master of theology from Emory University's Candler School of Theology. Jonathan resides outside of Atlanta, where he actively serves and teaches at Cross Pointe Church. He would love to connect with you at www.jonathanmerritt.com.

You can follow Jonathan, but please, only on Twitter: @jonathanmerritt.

Notes

Zero | Read This First

1. See Leonard Sweet and Frank Viola, *Jesus Manifesto: Restoring the Supremacy and Sovereignty of Jesus Christ* (Nashville, TN: Thomas Nelson, 2010), xvii. These writers have noted that the "you say" is contextual and concluded that it is a question each generation and culture has to answer. I agree with them, but we must also acknowledge that while the answer may be contextual, Peter's answer is timeless. So must ours be.
2. Matthew 16:16.
3. Hebrews 13:8.
4. Albert Schweitzer, *The Quest of the Historical Jesus: A Critical Study of Its Progress from Reimarus to Wrede*, trans. William Montgomery (1956; New York: Macmillan, 1961), 4.
5. For a complete look at this trend, see Jaroslav Pelikan's *Jesus through the Centuries: His Place in the History of Culture* (New Haven, CT: Yale University Press, 1985).
6. See Pelikan, *Jesus through the Centuries*.
7. Jacques Ellul, *The Subversion of Christianity* (Grand Rapids: William B. Eerdmans, 1986), 10–11.
8. Michelle A. Vu, "Evangelical Movement at 'Head-Snapping' Moment, Says Scholar," *The Christian Post*, Oct. 11, 2009, http://www.christianpost.com/news/evangelical-movement-at-head-snapping-moment-says-scholar-41337/.

One | Breakfast with Falwell

1. James Davison Hunter, *Culture Wars: The Struggle to Define America* (New York: Basic Books, 1992), 34.
2. Taken from my essay "Red, Blue, or Green?," in *Green Revolution: Coming Together to Care for Creation* by Ben Lowe (Deerfield, IL: Intervarsity Press, 2009), 164–165.
3. See Richard A. Horsley, *Jesus and Empire: The Kingdom of God and the New World Disorder* (Minneapolis: Fortress Press, 2002), 10–28.

4. The phrase appears more than 60 times in the New Testament alone, most often in the Gospels.
5. See Jesus' "Sermon on the Mount" in Matthew 5–7.
6. Colossians 1:15–20.
7. Mark 1:15.
8. Luke 17:21.
9. See Gregory A. Boyd, *The Myth of a Christian Nation: How the Quest for Political Power Is Destroying the Church* (Grand Rapids, MI: Zondervan, 2005), 11. For more on how many reform movements on the left and the right are tied up in the same assumptions, see Horsley, *Jesus and Empire*, 2ff.
10. Russell Moore, *The Kingdom of Christ: The New Evangelical Perspective* (Wheaton, IL: Crossway Books, 2004), 15. It is interesting in light of this observation to note that Jerry Falwell once said, "Moral Majority is a political organization and is not based on theological considerations."
11. As Gregory Boyd has pointed out, "Even more fundamentally, because this myth links the Kingdom of God with certain political stances within American politics, it has greatly compromised the holy beauty of the Kingdom of God to non-Christians." *The Myth of a Christian Nation*, 13.
12. Jerry Falwell, quoted in Richard John Neuhaus, *The Naked Public Square: Religion and Democracy in America* (Grand Rapids, MI: Eerdmans, 1986), 10.
13. C. S. Lewis, *Screwtape Letter—Special Illustrated Edition* (New York: HarperOne, 2009), 42.

Two | Journey to Montreat

1. A. M. Rosenthal, "On My Mind: Clinton's Bank Account," *New York Times*, April 2, 1993.
2. Frank Luntz, *What Americans Really Want—Really: The Truth about Our Hopes, Dreams, and Fears* (New York: Hyperion, 2009), 163.
3. David Kirkpatrick, "The 2004 Campaign: Strategy; Bush Allies Till Fertile Soil, among Baptists, for Votes," *New York Times*, June 18, 2004.
4. Andy Birkey, "Pulpit Freedom Sunday: Complaints Filed against Churches That Endorsed McCain," *Minnesota Independent*, September 29, 2008.
5. Ibid.
6. As cited in "Spotlight: Evangelical vs. Mainline Politics," *Christianity Today*, December 2010, 11, http://www.christianitytoday.com/ct/special/pdf/1122spotlightevangelicalmainline.pdf.

7. Robert H. Bork, *Slouching towards Gomorrah: Modern Liberalism and American Decline* (New York: Regan Books, 1997), 284.
8. Jim Wallis, *God's Politics: Why the Right Get It Wrong and the Left Doesn't Get It* (San Francisco: Harper San Francisco, 2006).
9. Sheryl Henderson Blunt, "Declaring Victory," *Christianity Today*, November 8, 2006, http://www.christianitytoday.com/ct/2006/nov emberweb-only/145-35.0.html.
10. Jordan Green, "Interview with Donald Miller," *Burnside Writers Blog*, September 25, 2008, http://burnsidewriterscollective.blogspot.com/2008/09/interview-with-donald-miller.html.
11. Ibid.
12. Michael Gerson and Peter Wehner, *City of Man: Religion and Politics in a New Era* (Chicago: Moody Publishers, 2010), 16.
13. When speculating on the question in electoral politics of "who is using whom," James Davison Hunter writes, "The obvious answer is to say that it is the candidates who cynically use the symbols of the culture war and thus one constituency or the other in the service of their own political ambitions." *Culture Wars: The Struggle to Define America* (New York: Basic Books, 1992), 286.
14. D. G. Hart, *That Old-Time Religion in Modern America* (Chicago: Ivan R. Dee, 2003), 27.
15. See Robert Wuthnow, *The Restructuring of American Religion* (Princeton, NJ: Princeton University Press, 1988).
16. David Kuo, *Tempting Faith: An Inside Story of Political Seduction* (New York: Free Press, 2006), 229–230.
17. Hunter, *Culture Wars*, 286.
18. Or as conservative writer Michael Gerson says, "The person they fall out with is not only on the wrong side of an issue; they are on the wrong side of God." *City of Man*, 30.
19. See Cal Thomas and Ed Dobson, *Blinded by Might: Can the Religious Right Save America?* (Grand Rapids, MI: Zondervan, 1999), 98–99.
20. Ross Douthat, "The Partisan Mind," *New York Times*, November 28, 2010.
21. Ibid.
22. Their title, not mine.
23. Taken from my article "The Uncertain Future of Evangelical Voters," *Washington Post* On Faith blog, November 2008.
24. For example, a *New York Times* exit poll proved my hunch right. Young evangelicals voted for Barack Obama in 2008 in twice the numbers they had voted for John Kerry in 2004.
25. Dan Cox, "Young White Evangelicals: Less Republican, Still Conservative," *The Pew Forum on Religion and Public Life*, September 28,

2007, http://pewforum.org/Politics-and-Elections/Young-White-Evan
gelicals-Less-Republican-Still-Conservative.aspx.

26. Timothy Keller, *The Reason for God* (New York: Dutton, 2008), xix–xx.
27. As the late Christian thinker Francis Schaeffer used to remind us.
28. Nancy Gibbs and Michael Duffy, *The Preacher and the Presidents: Billy Graham in the White House* (New York: Center Street, 2007), 132.
29. Nancy Gibbs and Michael Duffy, "President Obama Meets Billy Graham," *Time*, April 25, 2010, http://www.time.com/time/nation/article/0,8599,1984421,00.html.
30. Gibbs and Duffy, *The Preacher and the Presidents*, 31.
31. Gibbs and Duffy, "President Obama Meets Billy Graham."
32. Nancy Gibbs and Michael Duffy, "Billy Graham: A Spiritual Gift to All," *Time*, May 31, 2007, http://www.time.com/time/nation/article/0,8599,1627139,00.html.

Three | Christians at War

1. Jim VandeHei, "Pipeline to the President for GOP Conservatives," *Washington Post*, December 24, 2004, http://www.washingtonpost.com/wp-dyn/articles/A23206-2004Dec23.html.
2. Ibid.
3. This story was recounted by journalist Max Blumenthal in "The Christian Right's Humble Servant," *Alternet*, November 15, 2004, http://www.alternet.org/election04/20499/. It was later retold by Craig Unger in *The Fall of the House of Bush: The Untold Story of How a Band of True Believers Seized the Executive Branch, Started the Iraq War, and Still Imperils America's Future* (New York: Scribner, 2007).
4. "You Helped This Happen: Jerry Falwell and Pat Robertson React to the September 11 Terrorist Attacks on American Soil," Beliefnet, http://www.beliefnet.com/Faiths/Christianity/2001/09/You-Helped-This-Happen.aspx.
5. John 9:1–2.
6. Pastor Jud Wilhite draws a similar connection in his book *Torn: Trusting God When Life Leaves You in Pieces* (Colorado Springs: Multnomah, 2011), 101–109.
7. Press release from Jerry Falwell Ministries, September 18, 2001.
8. Days before Falwell's death, he told CNN's Christiane Amanpour that he stood by his original statement.
9. As quoted by Paul Froese and Christopher Bader, *America's Four Gods: What We Say about God—And What That Says about Us* (New York: Oxford University Press, 2010), 81.
10. Dated March 26, 2010. As quoted on *Countdown with Keith Olbermann*, January 13, 2011.

11. David Kinnaman and Gabe Lyons, *Unchristian: What a New Generation Really Thinks about Christianity... and Why It Matters* (Grand Rapids, MI: Baker Books, 2007).
12. Taken from my article "Incivility Muzzles Interactive Debate," *Atlanta Journal-Constitution*, August 22, 2009.
13. Taken from my article "Shooting Underscores Need for Civility," *WashingtonPost.com*, January 13, 2011, http://onfaith.washington post.com/onfaith/panelists/jonathan_merritt/2011/01/shooting _underscores_need_for_civility.html.
14. Peggy Noonan, *Patriotic Grace: What It Is and Why We Need It Now* (New York: HarperCollins, 2008).
15. See John Murray Cuddihy, *Ordeal of Civility: Freud, Marx, Levi-Strauss, and the Jewish Struggle with Modernity* (Boston, MA: Beacon Press, 1987).
16. For more on this idea, see Os Guinness's book *The Case for Civility: And Why Our Future Depends on It* (New York: HarperOne, 2008).
17. This story is told in more detail in my book *Green Like God: Unlocking the Divine Plan for Our Planet* (Nashville, TN: FaithWords, 2010).
18. Cal Thomas and Ed Dobson, *Blinded by Might: Can the Religious Right Save America?* (Grand Rapids, MI: Zondervan, 1999), 27.
19. Ibid., 34.
20. As quoted by Secretary of Defense Robert Gates at the Marine Corps Association Annual Dinner, July 18, 2007, http://www.defense.gov /speeches/speech.aspx?speechid=1170.

Four | Our Constant Temptation

1. Robert Louis Wilken, *The Christians as the Romans Saw Them* (New Haven, CT: Yale University Press, 2003), 117–125.
2. Michael Gerson and Peter Wehner, *City of Man: Religion and Politics in a New Era* (Chicago: Moody Publishers, 2010), 18.
3. Walter Wink, *The Powers That Be: Theology for a New Millennium* (New York: Three Rivers Press, 1999), 89–90.
4. Robert Bretall, ed., *A Kierkegaard Anthology* (Princeton, NJ: Princeton University Press, 1973), 397.
5. As historian Barry Hankins has pointed out, aligning theological and political commitments has been "endemic to evangelicalism since the early twentieth century." *Francis Schaeffer and the Shaping of Evangelical America* (Grand Rapids, MI: Eerdmans, 2008), 229.
6. As shown in figure 3.5 of Robert D. Putnam and David E. Campbell's *American Grace: How Religion Divides and Unites Us* (New York: Simon & Schuster, 2010), 84.

7. Ibid., 82.
8. Ibid., 87; emphasis added.
9. Sydney E. Ahlstrom, *A Religious History of the American People*, 2nd ed. (New Haven, CT: Yale University Press, 2004), 954–955.
10. Ibid.
11. Putnam and Campbell, *American Grace*, 97–98.
12. Amy Sullivan, "Young Evangelicals: Expanding Their Mission," *Time*, June 1, 2010.
13. Ross Douthat, "A Tough Season for Believers," *New York Times*, December 19, 2010, http://www.nytimes.com/2010/12/20/opinion /20douthat.html.
14. William Proctor, *The Gospel According to the New York Times: How the World's Most Powerful News Organization Shapes Your Mind and Values* (Nashville, TN: B&H Publishing Group, 2000), 33.
15. Putnam and Campbell, *American Grace*, 130.
16. Ibid., 120.
17. Ibid., 99.
18. Mainline Protestant denominations, which tend to be more liberal, have been bleeding for decades because of their blatant partisanship. John Richard Neuhaus once called mainline communities "sideline churches" because they had become culturally insignificant, partly because of their abandonment of orthodoxy and partly because they are "narrowly and predictably political." While most conservative Protestant congregations haven't fallen into the first trap, some are guilty of the last. If they become politically narrow and predictable, they may find themselves in a similar situation to that of mainline churches. In fact, the once-growing evangelical church has already started declining in America.
19. Scott McConnell, "LifeWay Research Finds Reasons 18-to-22-Year-Olds Drop Out of Church," August 7, 2007, LifeWay Research, http:// www.lifeway.com/Article/LifeWay-Research-finds-reasons-18-to -22-year-olds-drop-out-of-church.
20. Thom S. Rainer and Sam S. Rainer, *Essential Church? Reclaiming a Generation of Dropouts* (Nashville, TN: B&H Books, 2008), 23.
21. David Kinnaman and Gabe Lyons, *Unchristian: What a New Generation Really Thinks about Christianity...and Why It Matters* (Grand Rapids, MI: Baker Books, 2007), 27.
22. Ibid., 28, 30.
23. Ibid., 28.
24. Ibid., 26; emphasis in original.
25. The reactions and perceptions of the general public are pushing our country into a new moment that many have dubbed "post-Christian," a label intended to draw a distinction between our current moment

and the one my grandmother loved so dearly. In the words of Albert Mohler, president of Southern Baptist Theological Seminary, "The most basic contours of American culture have been altered. Clearly, there is a new narrative, a post-Christian narrative, that is animating large portions of this society." Jon Meacham, "The End of Christian America," *Newsweek*, April 13, 2009.

26. Ibid.
27. Kinnaman and Lyons, *Unchristian*, 153.
28. Tony Campolo, *Choose Love Not Power: How to Right the World's Wrongs from a Place of Weakness* (Ventura, CA: Regal, 2009), back of the book.
29. John 18:33.
30. John 18:36.
31. See Gregory A. Boyd, *The Myth of a Christian Nation: How the Quest for Political Power Is Destroying the Church* (Grand Rapids, MI: Zondervan, 2005), 27.
32. Matthew 22:21.
33. Luke 22:50–51.
34. Boyd, *The Myth of a Christian Nation*, 28.
35. As quoted by Leonard Sweet and Frank Viola, *Jesus Manifesto: Restoring the Supremacy and Sovereignty of Jesus Christ* (Nashville, TN: Thomas Nelson, 2010), 91.
36. This story is paraphrased from 2 Kings 20:12–15.
37. 2 Kings 20:16–18.
38. 2 Kings 20:19 NLT.
39. As quoted in Diana Kendall, *Sociology in Our Times: The Essentials* (Florence, KY: Wadsworth Publishing, 2011), 234.

Five | A Symphony of Voices

1. "New Barna Study Explores Current Views on Abortion," The Barna Group, June 14, 2010, http://www.barna.org/culture-articles/394-new-barna-study-explores-current-views-on-abortion-.
2. As has been reported extensively by polling organizations such as Barna Research Group and Pew Forum on Religion and Public Life.
3. As quoted in Gabe Lyons, "The Good News about the End of Christian America," *Washington Post*, October 5, 2010, http://onfaith.washingtonpost.com/onfaith/guestvoices/2010/10/the_good_news_about_the_end_of_christian_america.html.
4. LifeWay Research.
5. Proverbs 6:16–19.
6. Rev. Tyler Wigg-Stevenson, "Hiroshima and the Transfiguration: A Meditation," Franciscan Associates, August 6, 2010, http://francis

canassociates.wordpress.com/2010/08/06/hiroshima-and-the-transfig
uration-a-meditation-by-rev-tyler-wigg-stevenson/.
7. "Who We Are," International Justice Mission, www.ijm.org/who
-we-are.
8. Bethany Hoang, "Picture Justice: Embracing Our Global Neighborhood," Q, http://www.qideas.org/essays/picture-justice-embracing-our
-global-neighborhood.aspx.
9. As William McKenzie of the *Dallas Morning News* has stated, this is
more than a generational shift. It is a thematic shift affecting many
Christians both young and old. See William McKenzie, "Younger
Evangelicals Taking Movement in a New Direction," *Dallas Morning
News*, March 18, 2008.
10. David Gushee, *The Future of Faith in Politics* (Waco, TX: Baylor University Press, 2008).
11. Matthew 22:16–17.
12. Matthew 22:20–21.
13. David A. Graham, "Faces of the Christian Right: Leaders of a Changing Movement," *Newsweek*, December 8, 2010.
14. Haley Edwards, "Young, Evangelical…for Obama?," *Seattle Times*,
May 11, 2008.
15. 1 Corinthians 12:12–21.

Six | Faith at the Seams

1. I had never heard this quote before, but after doing some research
realized he had quoted Falwell verbatim. See "A Gay Activist School
Pal Calls Jerry Falwell's Bluff in Court," *People* 23, no. 16 (October
14, 1985), http://www.people.com/people/archive/article/0,,20091945
,00.html.
2. Jonathan Merritt, "Evangelical Shift on Gays: Why Clobber Scriptures Are Losing Ground," *Christian Science Monitor*, March 2011.
3. See Jonathan Merritt, "An Evangelical's Plea: 'Love the Sinner,'" *USA
Today*, April 22, 2009.
4. *Intelligence Report* magazine, http://www.splcenter.org/intel/intel
report/article.jsp?pid=868; and the Southern Poverty Law Center,
http://www.splcenter.org/intel/intelreport/article.jsp?aid=522.
5. E. Calvin Beisner, "AIDS and Rationality," http://www.ecalvinbeisner
.com/freearticles/AidsandRationality.pdf.
6. Tony Perkins, "Christian Compassion Requires the Truth about
Harms of Homosexuality," *Washington Post*, October 11, 2010,
http://onfaith.washingtonpost.com/onfaith/guestvoices/2010/10
/christian_compassion_requires_the_truth_about_harms_of_homo
sexuality.html.

7. David Barton, "Homosexuals in the Military," WallBuilders, 2001, http://www.wallbuilders.com/LIBissuesArticles.asp?id=101. It's important to note that the actions Barton attributes to Washington and Jefferson have been contested by others.

8. Karl Frisch, "Beck Confidant Barton Wonders Why We Don't 'Regulate Homosexuality' Like Trans Fats," Media Matters, October 7, 2010, http://mediamatters.org/blog/201010070023.

9. 1 John 3:16–19.

10. "Warning Signs of Suicide," The Trevor Project, http://www.thetrevor project.org/suicide-resources/warning-signs.

11. Kristen Moulton, "Survey Links Gay Suicides to Religious Messages," Salt Lake Tribune, October 22, 2010, http://www.sltrib .com/sltrib/50518515-76/americans-church-faith-gave.html.csp.

12. Public Religion Research, "20 Years of Polling on Gay and Lesbian Issues from Pew," August 20, 2010, http://publicreligion.org /newsroom/2010/08/news-release-20-years-of-polling-on-gay -lesbian-issues-from-pew/.

13. David Kinnaman and Gabe Lyons, Unchristian: What a New Generation Really Thinks about Christianity . . . and Why It Matters (Grand Rapids, MI: Baker Books, 2007).

14. Public Religion Research, "The Faith and American Politics Survey: The Young and the Faithful," 2008, http://publicreligion.org /research/2008/10/faith-in-american-politics-survey/.

15. John Shore, "'Just Resist the Temptation': The Anti-love Approach to Homosexuality," Huffington Post, October 2, 2010, http://www .huffingtonpost.com/john-shore/how-is-being-gay-like-glu_b _747071.html.

16. 1 Corinthians 13:4–5 NLT.

17. See Jonathan Merritt, "An Evangelical's Plea, 'Love the Sinner,'" USA Today, April 22, 2009.

18. For example, Focus on the Family said it "opposed efforts to protect gay kids from bullying because those programs promote acceptance of homosexuality as normal." Source: American Values Survey, Public Religion Research Institute, 2010.

19. Karen Auge, "Suicides of Bullied Gay Kids in Other States Jolt Colorado Educators to Action," Denver Post, October 12, 2010, http:// www.denverpost.com/technology/ci_16314707; emphasis added.

20. Public Religion Research, "The Faith and American Politics Survey: The Young and the Faithful," 2008, http://publicreligion.org /research/2008/10/faith-in-american-politics-survey/.

21. From an unpublished interview I conducted with Robert Jones of Public Religion Research in March 2011.

22. Pew Research Center, "Most Still Oppose Gay Marriage, but Support for Civil Unions Continues to Rise," October 9, 2009, http://pew research.org/pubs/1375/gay-marriage-civil-unions-opinion.
23. In Frederica Mathewes-Green, *Gender: Men, Women, Sex, Feminism* (Ben Lomond, CA: Conciliar Press, 2002), 166.

Seven | Give Me the Songs of a Nation

1. Some minority, female, and younger voices were added after the document was released.
2. Taken from my article "Manhattan Declaration Unlikely to Inspire Young Christians," WashingtonPost.com, November 24, 2009.
3. Laurie Goodstein, "Christian Leaders Unite on Political Issues," *New York Times*, November 20, 2009.
4. Mark I. Pinsky, "The Truth about Evangelicals," *USA Today*, September 18, 2011, http://www.usatoday.com/news/opinion/forum /story/2011-09-18/evangelical-christians-republicans/50457192/1.
5. Cal Thomas and Ed Dobson, *Blinded by Might: Can the Religious Right Save America?* (Grand Rapids, MI: Zondervan, 1999).
6. See David Kinnaman, "Rethinking and Re-engaging Missions," *Rev Magazine*, July/August 2009, http://www.rev.org/article.asp?ID= 3312.
7. For more discussion of this, see "The New Evangelical Scandal," by Matthew Lee Anderson, in *The City*, Winter 2008, http://www .civitate.org/2009/01/the-new-evangelical-scandal/.
8. James 4:17.
9. This quote can be found any number of places in print and electronic media attributed to Winston Churchill, but it is important to note that research argues against such a claim (see Ralph Keyes, *Nice Guys Finish Seventh: False Phrases, Spurious Sayings and Familiar Misquotations*). Additionally, the Churchill Centre says on its website, "There is no record of anyone hearing Churchill say this."
10. See the chapter titled, "Provoked, Not Offended" in Gabe Lyons, *The Next Christians: The Good News about the End of Christian America* (New York: Doubleday Religion, 2010).
11. Philip Yancey, *The Jesus I Never Knew* (Grand Rapids, MI: Zondervan, 1995), 75–76.
12. Thomas and Dobson, *Blinded by Might*, 74.
13. Sociologist D. Michael Lindsay confirms the influence of this thinking in his book *Faith in the Halls of Power: How Evangelicals Joined the American Elite* (New York: Oxford University Press, 2007), arguing that Christians have moved from protest mode—casting stones at anyone hostile to a Christian worldview—to engagement mode— producing good art, better products, and strong ideas that compete in

and shape the marketplace (http://www.ttf.org/index/journal/detail
/what-do-evangelicals-do-with-power).
14. This is what Scot McKnight refers to as the "read and retrieve"
method in his influential book on this subject, *The Blue Parakeet:
Rethinking How You Read the Bible* (Grand Rapids, MI: Zondervan,
2008).
15. Polling by the Pew Forum on Religion and Public Life shows that the
number of "young evangelicals" who claim to be "biblical literalists"
has not wavered since 1984.
16. One might argue that the climax for many, including previous generations, has been found in a pre-tribulational rapture or, for Christians
who find their identity rooted in more Calvinistic traditions, in the
letters of Paul.
17. As Leonard Sweet and Frank Viola point out in their book *Jesus Manifesto*, every awakening in the history of the church includes both a
"rediscovery of the 'living Word,' or the Scriptures and its authority"
and "a rediscovery of the living Christ and His supremacy." *Jesus
Manifesto: Restoring the Supremacy and Sovereignty of Jesus Christ*
(Nashville, TN: Thomas Nelson, 2010), xvii.
18. 1 Corinthians 15:3.
19. Lyons, *The Next Christians*, 56.
20. Union University, "Moore Connects Adoption to the Gospel During
Crabtree Lecture Series," April 7, 2011, http://www.uu.edu/news
/release.cfm?ID=1826.
21. Dan Gilgoff, "Can a Culture War Manifesto Reach a New Generation of Evangelicals and Catholics?," *US News* God and Country
blog, November 20, 2009, http://www.usnews.com/news/blogs/god
-and-country/2009/11/20/can-a-culture-war-manifesto-reach-a-new
-generation-of-evangelicals-and-catholics.
22. Taken from my article "Manhattan Declaration Unlikely to Inspire
Young Christians," *Washington Post* On Faith blog, November 24,
2009, http://onfaith.washingtonpost.com/onfaith/guestvoices/2009/11
/manhattan_declaration_unlikely_to_inspire_young_christians.html.

Eight | A Touch Closer

1. Matthew 7:29.
2. 1 John 2:5–6 NLT.
3. Julie Pace, "Obama Speaks at Notre Dame," Associated Press, May
17, 2009, http://www.wane.com/dpps/news/national/midwest/Obama
_speaks_at_Notre_Dame_20090517_2422191.
4. See Jonathan Merritt, "The Possibilities of Abortion Reduction,"
Reject Apathy, http://rejectapathy.com/loss-of-innocents/features
/18322-abortion-reduction.

5. Ibid.
6. Samuel Rodriguez, a pro-life supporter of abortion reduction and president of the National Hispanic Christian Leadership Conference, responded to these criticisms in my article "The Possibilities of Abortion Reduction" for *Reject Apathy*:

   > The criticisms of abortion reduction strategies are an extension of the archaic modus operandi of the Christian right. It is a political ideology rather than a religious ethos ideology. The religious right became a de facto extension of the Republican Party. As a result, anyone who is moved to work with those outside of that party is seen as acquiescing. I get attacked from the extreme Right and they say I am selling out, and yet I am more committed to our values than ever. We can find common ground without compromising any of our core values.

7. Sarah Posner, "Incrementalism Masquerading as Progressivism," *American Prospect*, January 15, 2009, http://prospect.org/article /incrementalism-masquerading-progressivism.
8. See Ephesians 4:12.
9. John R. W. Stott, *The Radical Disciple* (Nottingham: InterVarsity Press, 2010).
10. John 12:2–3.
11. Luke 10:41–42.
12. 2 Corinthians 2:14; emphasis added.
13. As Leonard Sweet and Frank Viola write in *Jesus Manifesto: Restoring the Supremacy and Sovereignty of Jesus Christ* (Nashville, TN: Thomas Nelson, 2010):

   > In Bethany, Jesus Christ is valued for His exceeding worth. There is nothing too costly to lay at his feet. When the flask is broken, the house surrendered to the aroma of the perfume. Herein lies a great truth: When the vessel is broken, the fragrance of Christ pours forth.

Nine | One Hundred Pianos

1. *Charisma Magazine* ran an article in August 2007 showcasing the inner musings of college and graduate students across the United States titled "God on Campus," by Suzy Richardson. Their criticisms range from the church "trying so hard to be relevant bastions of spiritual depth that they are missing the integral element of Christianity: love" to "stuck in tradition and practice" to "suffer[ing] from a lack of passion and new ideas to pursue the very mission of Jesus—to seek and save the lost."
2. "Race on *The Oprah Show*: A 25-Year Look Back," *Oprah Winfrey Show*, January 17, 2011, http://www.oprah.com/oprahshow/Race-on-The-Oprah-Show-A-25-Year-Look-Back/.

3. Shane Claiborne and Jonathan Wilson-Hartgrove, *Becoming the Answer to Our Prayers: Prayer for Ordinary Radicals* (Downers Grove, IL: IVP Books, 2008), 79.
4. John 17:11.
5. Ephesians 6:12.
6. A. W. Tozer, *The Pursuit of God: The Human Thirst for the Divine* (Camp Hill, PA: Wingspread Publishers), 90.
7. As historian Mark Noll has pointed out, "Religion has always been crucial for the workings of race in politics." *God and Race in American Politics: A Short History* (Princeton, NJ: Princeton University Press, 2010), 1. He goes on to say that "a Christianity mostly bereft of its antebellum social vitality played a major part in sanctioning systemic white discrimination against African-Americans."
8. Anne Lamott, *Traveling Mercies: Some Thoughts on Faith* (New York: Pantheon, 1999).
9. So strong was this division that the General Assembly of the Presbyterian Church in the Confederate States of America recognized in 1864, "We hesitate not to affirm that it is the peculiar mission of the Southern Baptist Church to conserve the institution of slavery." Ernest Trice Thompson, *Presbyterians in the South*, vol. 2, 1861–1890 (Richmond, VA: John Knox, 1973), 61–62.
10. As quoted in Steven Wise, *An American Trilogy: Death, Slavery, and Dominion on the Banks of the Cape Fear River* (Philadelphia: Da Capo Press, 2009), 203.
11. As Mark Noll notes,
    Moreover, if the combination of black religious self-assertion and broad governmental action led to genuine progress in some aspects of civil rights, it also led to significant political conflict, especially when white evangelical Christians and some Roman Catholics, even as they accommodated themselves to black civil rights, mobilized for political action because of offense at the expansion of governmental authority. *God and Race in American Politics*, 176–177.
12. For more on this, see Stephen R. Haynes, *Noah's Curse: The Biblical Justification of American Slavery* (New York: Oxford University Press, 2002).
13. Ken Walker, "Vacation Bible School Wars: Critics Say SBC Curriculum about Asia Is 'Racially Offensive,'" *Christianity Today*, March 1, 2004, http://www.christianitytoday.com/ct/2004/march/29.26.html.
14. Austin Chee, "A Public Apology to Our Asian American Brothers and Sisters," March 14, 2007, http://whyismarko.com/2007/a-public-apology-to-our-asian-american-brothers-and-sisters/.

15. Robert Wuthnow, *After the Baby Boomers: How Twenty- and Thirty-Somethings Are Shaping the Future of American Religion* (Princeton, NJ: Princeton University Press, 2007), 183. Wuthnow goes on to note, "No consideration of the future of American religion is thus complete without focusing on these new immigrants."
16. Soong-Chan Rah, *The Next Evangelicalism: Freeing the Church from Western Cultural Captivity* (Downers Grove, IL: InterVarsity Press, 2009), 74.
17. As Mark Noll writes, "The American political system and the American practice of Christianity, which have provided so much good for so many years, have never been able to overcome race." *God and Race in American Politics*, 178.

Ten | The Burden of Every Generation

1. Richard Mouw, "Carl Henry Was Right," *Christianity Today*, January 27, 2010; emphasis added.
2. Ibid; emphasis added.
3. As Michael Gerson and Peter Wehner write in *City of Man: Religion and Politics in a New Era* (Chicago: Moody Publishers, 2010), 36:
   The role of the church, at least as we interpret it, is to provide individual Christians with a moral framework through which they can work out their duties as citizens and engage the world in a thoughtful way, even as it resists the temptation to instruct them on how to do their job or on which specific public policies they ought to embrace.
4. Jerry Falwell, interview with Don Carleton at Liberty University, October 16, 2003, video available at http://www.emmytvlegends.org/interviews/people/jerry-falwell.
5. Cathleen Falsani, "Sigh of Relief over Falwell's Death," *Chicago Sun-Times*, May 18, 2007.

Selected Bibliography

Bakker, Jay. *Fall to Grace: A Revolution of God, Self, and Society.* Nashville, TN: FaithWords, 2011.

Bakker, Jay. *Son of a Preacher Man: My Search for Grace in the Shadows.* New York: HarperCollins, 2001.

Bauckham, Richard. *The Bible in Politics: How to Read the Bible Politically.* Louisville, KY: Westminster John Knox Press, 2011.

Belz, Joel, and Marvin Olasky. *Whirled Views: Tracking Today's Culture Storms.* Westchester, IL: Crossway Books, 1997.

Benne, Robert. *Good and Bad Ways to Think about Religion and Politics.* Grand Rapids, MI: Eerdmans, 2010.

Blue, Kevin. *Practical Justice: Living Off-Center in a Self-Centered World.* Downers Grove, IL: InterVarsity Press, 2006.

Boyd, Gregory A. *The Myth of a Christian Nation: How the Quest for Political Power Is Destroying the Church.* Grand Rapids, MI: Zondervan, 2005.

Campolo, Tony. *Red Letter Christians: A Citizen's Guide to Faith & Politics.* Ventura, CA: Regal Books, 2008.

Cannon, Mae Elise. *Social Justice Handbook: Small Steps for a Better World.* Downers Grove, IL: InterVarsity Press, 2009.

Carroll, Colleen. *The New Faithful: Why Young Adults Are Embracing Christian Orthodoxy.* Chicago: Loyola Press, 2002.

Carter, Craig A. *Rethinking Christ and Culture: A Post-Christendom Perspective.* Grand Rapids, MI: Brazos Press, 2007.

Claiborne, Shane, and Chris Haw. *Jesus for President: Politics for Ordinary Radicals.* Grand Rapids, IL: Zondervan, 2008.

Clapp, Rodney. *A Peculiar People: The Church as Culture in a Post-Christian Society.* Downers Grove, IL: InterVarsity Press, 1996.

Clawson, Julie. *Everyday Justice: The Global Impact of Our Daily Choices.* Downers Grove, IL: InterVarsity Press, 2009.

Cox, Harvey. *The Future of Faith.* New York: HarperCollins, 2009.

Crouch, Andy. *Culture Making: Recovering Our Creative Calling.* Downers Grove: InterVarsity Press, 2008.

Cunningham, Sarah. *Dear Church: Letters from a Disillusioned Generation*. Grand Rapids, MI: Zondervan, 2006.

Curry, Dean C. *A World Without Tyranny: Christian Faith and International Politics*. Westchester, IL: Crossway Books, 1990.

Dark, David. *The Gospel According to America: A Meditation of a God-Blessed, Christ-Haunted Idea*. Louisville, KY: Westminster John Knox Press, 2005.

De Marchi, Scott, and James T. Hamilton. *You Are What You Choose: The Habits of Mind That Really Determine How We Make Decisions*. New York: Portfolio, 2009.

Dochuk, Darren. *From Bible Belt to Sunbelt: Plain-Folk Religion, Grassroots Politics, and the Rise of Evangelical Conservatism*. New York: W. W. Norton, 2010.

D'Souza, Dinesh. *Letters to a Young Conservative*. New York: Basic Books, 2002.

Ellul, Jacques. *The Subversion of Christianity*. Grand Rapids, MI: Eerdmans, 1986.

Fiorina, Morris P., with Samual J. Abrams and Jeremy C. Pope. *Culture War? The Myth of a Polarized America*. New York: Pearson Longman, 2005.

Forster, Greg. *The Contested Public Square: The Crisis of Christianity and Politics*. Downers Grove, IL: IVP Academic, 2008.

Frost, Michael. *Exiles: Living Missionally in a Post-Christian Culture*. Peabody, MA: Hendrickson, 2006.

Garrison, Becky. *Red and Blue God, Black and Blue Church: Eyewitness Accounts of How American Churches Are Hijacking Jesus, Bagging the Beatitudes, and Worshipping the Almighty Dollar*. San Francisco: Wiley, 2006.

George, Robert P. *Clash of Orthodoxies: Law, Religion, and Morality in Crisis*. Wilmington, DE: Intercollegiate Studies Institute, 2002.

Gerson, Michael, and Peter Wehner. *The Powers That Be: Theology for a New Millennium*. Chicago: Moody Publishers, 2010.

Gilgoff, Dan. *The Jesus Machine: How James Dobson, Focus on the Family, and Evangelical America Are Winning the Culture War*. New York: St. Martin's Press, 2007.

Goldberg, Steven. *Bleached Faith: The Tragic Cost When Religion Is Forced into the Public Square*. Stanford, CA: Stanford Law Books, 2008.

Gottlieb, Roger S. *A Greener Faith: Religious Environmentalism and Our Planet's Future*. New York: Oxford University Press, 2006.

Grudem, Wayne. *Politics According to the Bible: A Comprehensive Resource for Understanding Modern Political Issues in Light of Scripture*. Grand Rapids, MI: Zondervan, 2010.

Guinness, Os. *The Case for Civility: And Why Our Future Depends on It*. San Francisco: HarperOne, 2008.

Gushee, David. *The Future of Faith in Politics: The Public Witness of the Evangelical Center*. Waco, TX: Baylor University Press, 2008.

Gushee, David, ed. *Christians and Politics beyond the Culture Wars: An Agenda for Engagement*. Grand Rapids, MI: Baker Books, 2000.

Gutenson, Charles. *Christians and the Common Good: How Faith Intersects with Public Life*. Grand Rapids, MI: Brazos Press, 2011.

Hankins, Barry. *Jesus and Gin: Evangelicalism, the Roaring Twenties and Today's Culture Wars*. New York: Palgrave Macmillan, 2010.

Harper, Lisa Sharon. *Evangelical Does Not Equal Republican...or Democrat*. New York: New Press, 2008.

Hart, D. G. *That Old-Time Religion in Modern America*. Chicago: Ivan R. Dee, 2003.

Haugen, Gary A. *Good News about Injustice*. Downers Grove, IL: InterVarsity Press, 1999.

Horsley, Richard A. *Jesus and Empire: The Kingdom of God and the New World Disorder*. Minneapolis: Fortress Press, 2002.

Horton, Michael. *Beyond Culture Wars: Is America a Mission Field or a Battlefield?* Chicago: Moody Publishers, 1994.

Hughes, Richard T. *Christian America and the Kingdom of God*. Urbana: University of Illinois Press, 2009.

Hunter, James Davison. *Culture Wars: The Struggle to Define America*. New York: Basic Books, 1992.

Hunter, James Davison. *To Change the World: The Irony, Tragedy, and Possibility of Christianity in the Late Modern World*. New York: Oxford University Press, 2010.

Hunter, Joel. *A New Kind of Conservative*. Ventura, CA: Regal Books, 2008.

Jenkins, Philip. *The Next Christendom: The Coming of Global Christianity*. New York: Oxford University Press, 2007.

Keller, Timothy. *Generous Justice: How God's Grace Makes Us Just*. New York: Dutton, 2010.

Kinnaman, David, and Gabe Lyons. *Unchristian: What a New Generation Really Thinks about Christianity...and Why It Matters*. Grand Rapids, MI: Baker Books, 2007.

Koyzis, David T. *Political Visions and Illusions: A Survey and Christian Critique of Contemporary Ideologies*. Downers Grove, IL: InterVarsity Press, 2003.

Kreeft, Peter. *How to Win the Culture War: A Christian Battle Plan for a Society in Crisis*. Downers Grove, IL: InterVarsity Press, 2002.

Kuitert, H. M. *Everything Is Politics, But Politics Is Not Everything*. Grand Rapids, MI: Eerdmans, 1986.

Land, Richard D. *The Divided States of America*. Nashville, TN: Thomas Nelson, 2008.

Lewis, C. S. *The Abolition of Man*. San Francisco: HarperOne, 2001.

Lewis, C. S. *The Screwtape Letters*. Uhrichsville, OH: Barbour Publishing, 1990.

Lindsay, Michael. *Faith in the Halls of Power: How Evangelicals Joined the American Elite*. New York: Oxford University Press, 2007.

Lyons, Gabe. *The Next Christians: The Good News about the End of Christian America*. New York: Doubleday Religious, 2010.

Marin, Andrew. *Love Is an Orientation: Elevating the Conversation with the Gay Community*. Downers Grove, IL: InterVarsity Press, 2009.

Marsden, George M. *Fundamentalism and American Culture*. New York: Oxford University Press, 2006.

Mathewes-Green, Frederica. *Gender: Men, Women, Sex, Feminism*. Ben Lomond, CA: Conciliar Press, 2002.

Meacham, Jon. *American Gospel: God, the Founding Fathers, and the Making of a Nation*. New York: Random House, 2006.

Mohler, R. Albert. *Culture Shift: Engaging Current Issues with Timeless Truth*. New York: Doubleday Religious, 2008.

Monsma, Stephen V. *Healing for a Broken World: Christian Perspectives on Public Policy*. Wheaton, IL: Crossway Books, 2008.

Monsma, Stephen V. *Pursuing Justice in a Sinful World*. Grand Rapids, MI: Eerdmans, 1984.

Moore, Russell D. *The Kingdom of Christ: The New Evangelical Perspective*. Wheaton, IL: Crossway Books, 2004.

Mouw, Richard J. *When the Kings Come Marching In: Isaiah and the New Jerusalem*. Grand Rapids, MI: Eerdmans, 2002.

Niebuhr, H. Richard. *Christ and Culture*. New York: Harper & Row, 1951.

Noll, Mark. *God and Race in American Politics: A Short History*. Princeton, NJ: Princeton University Press, 2010.

Noll, Mark, *The Scandal of the Evangelical Mind*. Grand Rapids, MI: Eerdmans, 1994.

Noll, Mark, and Luke Harlow, eds. *Religion and American Politics: From the Colonial Period to the Present*. 2nd ed. New York: Oxford University Press, 2007.

Olsen, Roger. *How to Be Evangelical Without Being Conservative*. Grand Rapids, MI: Zondervan, 2008.

Peterson, Brenda. *I Want to Be Left Behind: Finding Rapture Here on Earth*. Cambridge, MA: Da Capo Press, 2010.

Putnam, Robert, and David E. Campbell. *American Grace: How Religion Divides and Unites Us*. New York: Simon & Schuster, 2010.

Rah, Soong-Chan. *The Next Evangelicalism: Freeing the Church from Western Cultural Captivity.* Downers Grove, IL: InterVarsity Press, 2009.

Roose, Kevin. *The Unlikely Disciple: A Sinner's Semester at America's Holiest University.* New York: Grand Central Publishing, 2009.

Schaeffer, Francis. *A Christian Manifesto.* Westchester, IL: Crossway Books, 2005.

Shiflett, Dave. *Exodus: Why Americans Are Fleeing Liberal Churches for Conservative Christianity.* New York: Penguin, 2005.

Sider, Ronald J. *Rich Christians in an Age of Hunger: Moving from Affluence to Generosity.* Nashville, TN: Thomas Nelson, 2005.

Sider, Ronald J. *The Scandal of Evangelical Politics: Why Are Christians Missing the Chance to Really Change the World?* Grand Rapids, MI: Baker Books, 2008.

Stark, Rodney. *The Rise of Christianity: How the Obscure, Marginal Jesus Movement Became the Dominant Religious Force in the Western World in a Few Centuries.* New York: HarperCollins, 2006.

Stark, Rodney. *What Americans Really Believe.* Waco, TX: Baylor University Press, 2008.

Stassen, Glen H., and David Gushee. *Kingdom Ethics: Following Jesus in Contemporary Context.* Downers Grove, IL: IVP Academic, 2003.

Stetzer, Ed. *Lost and Found.* Nashville, TN: Broadman & Holman Publishing, 2009.

Sullivan, Amy. *The Party Faithful: How and Why Democrats Are Closing the God Gap.* New York: Scribner, 2008.

Taylor, Adam. *Mobilizing Hope: Faith-Inspired Activism for a Post-Civil Rights Generation.* Downers Grove, IL: InterVarsity Press, 2010.

Tennent, Timothy C. *Theology in the Context of World Christianity: How the Global Church Is Influencing the Way We Think about and Discuss Theology.* Grand Rapids, MI: Zondervan, 2007.

Thomas, Cal, and Ed Dobson. *Blinded by Might: Can the Religious Right Save America?* Grand Rapids, MI: Zondervan, 2000.

Thompson, Chad W. *Loving Homosexuals as Jesus Would: A Fresh Christian Approach.* Grand Rapids, IL: Brazos Press, 2004.

Townsend, Kathleen Kennedy. *Failing America's Faithful: How Today's Churches Are Mixing God with Politics and Losing Their Way.* New York: Grand Central Publishing, 2007.

Trueman, Carl R. *Republocrat: Confessions of a Liberal Conservative.* Phillipsburg, NJ: P&R Publishing, 2010.

VanDrunen, David. *Living in Two Kingdoms: A Biblical Vision for Christianity and Culture.* Westchester, IL: Crossway Books, 2010.

Via, Dan O., and Robert A. J. Gagnon. *Homosexuality and the Bible: Two Views.* Minneapolis: Augsburg Fortress Press, 2003.

Volf, Miroslav. *A Public Faith: How Followers of Christ Should Serve the Common Good*. Grand Rapids, MI: Brazos Press, 2011.

Webb, William J. *Slaves, Women, and Homosexuals: Exploring the Hermeneutics of Cultural Analysis*. Downers Grove, IL: InterVarsity Press, 2001.

Wilken, Robert Louis. *The Christians as the Romans Saw Them*. New Haven, CT: Yale University Press, 2003.

Wilkens, Steve, and Don Thorsen. *Everything You Know about Evangelicals Is Wrong (Well, Almost Everything)*. Grand Rapids, MI: Baker Books, 2010.

Williams, Daniel. *God's Own Party: The Making of the Christian Right*. New York: Oxford University Press, 2010.

Wink, Walter. *The Powers That Be: Theology for a New Millennium*. New York: Three Rivers Press, 1999.

Wright, Bradley R. E. *Christians Are Hate-Filled Hypocrites...and Other Lies You've Been Told: A Sociologist Shatters Myths from the Secular and Christian Media*. Grand Rapids, MI: Bethany House, 2010.

Wuthnow, Robert. *After the Baby Boomers: How Twenty- and Thirty-Somethings Are Shaping the Future of American Religion*. Princeton, NJ: Princeton University Press, 2007.

Yoder, John Howard. *The Politics of Jesus*. 2nd ed. Grand Rapids, MI: Eerdmans, 1972.

Zoba, Wendy Murray. *The Beliefnet Guide to Evangelical Christianity*. New York: Doubleday, 2005.

Green Like God

by Jonathan Merritt

Accompany one pilgrim on a spiritual expedition from enviro-ambivalence to standing at the forefront of the green movement in the church. Jonathan Merritt confronts tough questions dividing America and the faith community while exploring God's plan for restoration. He shares his journey in the hope that you, too, will unlock the divine plan for our planet.

"Merritt's conversion may not change the world quite as much as [the apostle] Paul's, but he has changed his classroom epiphany into Topic A within...the biggest Protestant body in the U.S."

—*Time*